IN THE SPIRIT OF CHRISTMAS

THANKSGIVING

ADVENT

EPIPHANY

Selections for Daily Use
prepared by
New Hope Church Family And Friends

LEGACY HOUSE

Canoga Park, California

The cover, by Robert Wilkinson and David Coven,
is dedicated to Pastor Philip Assink
and his generosity of Spirit.

Edited by Lois Daily

The publisher has attempted to locate and secure
permission to reprint copyright material in this
book. If any acknowledgments have been omitted,
the publisher would appreciate receiving the
information so that proper credit may be given.

Printed in the United States of America

Library of Congress Cataloging-in-Publication Data

In the spirit of Christmas.

   1. Christmas–Meditations.   2. Thanksgiving Day–
Meditations.   3. Advent–Meditations.   4. Epiphany
season–Meditations.   I. New Hope Church (Canoga Park,
Los Angeles, Calif.)
BV45.I52   1987   242'.2   87-26059
ISBN 0-944741-00-2

The People Of God Declare His Glory

New Hope Community Church
22222 Saticoy Street
Canoga Park, California 91303

Introduction

THE FIRST CHRISTMAS GIFT was the Child himself. All other celebrations should be rooted in a response to that great Gift. Instead, people appear to be obsessed with outdoing the gifts that were first recorded as gold, frankincense and myrrh.

On the holiday stage covered with tinsel, glitter and flashing colored lights, this collection of meditations is humbly laid. The presumed goal is to link several holidays through reflective devotions, inspiring a search more diligent than that undertaken by the wisemen and uncovering a treasure more precious than gold. The hope is not only to recover the spiritual roots upon which these celebrations are based but also to help people branch out in their faith reaching new heights and horizons.

In The Spirit of Christmas begins with the United States custom of celebrating Thanksgiving on the fourth Thursday of November. This is rooted in the early history of settlers coming in the 1600's. As they concluded the long harvest season, they paused with their new native American friends to give thanks. They thanked the Creator for his faithful and abundant provision which would assure them of food for the winter.

Next, the Advent season of the church year, is a time not only to remember and celebrate the first coming of Jesus, but also to prepare for his second coming.

Christmas, of course, is the heart of the celebration. God sent his Son into the world that we might know his love and forgiveness.

Finally, we move on to celebrate Epiphany. Traditionally, this has been known as the day the three wisemen met the Christ-child. It gives us the opportunity to remember that December 25 is the beginning, not the end, of our Christmas celebration.

This book shares the beauty of the body of Christ. No one piece stands out above all the others. It is an intricate tapestry, woven from the fabric of the lives of God's people. Its strength is in its diversity. As you journey through, some thoughts will be more in tune with your own than others. You will recognize the beauty of God's people pouring out their hearts to bring healing, hope, and wholeness to you. It also helps us to remember that the holiday season is not just a reflection on past historical tradition, but a celebration of life today and hope for tomorrow. In the spirit of celebrating today, we have included new words and songs next to traditional thoughts and melodies. The hope for tomorrow is what we trust will be written on your heart as we join together in *The Spirit of Christmas*.

The philosophy of ministry statement of New Hope Community Church states, "We are believers on the way…" We invite you to share in our spiritual journey or pilgrimage, by using this gift from our church family to you. We trust it will help you see more clearly God's special Gift for us all.

Pastor Phil

PREFACE

In The Spirit of Christmas

"In the last days, God says,
I will pour out my Spirit on all people.
Your sons and daughters will prophesy,
  your young men will see visions,
  your old men will dream dreams.
Even on my servants, both men and
  women,
  I will pour out my Spirit in those days,
  and they will prophesy."

Acts 2:16–18
Joel 2:28, 29

Special friends of ours lovingly call it "chutzpadik." (This means to have incredible gall, brazen nerve, arrogance—such as no other word in no other language can do justice to.)*

The Joys of Yiddish by Leo Rosten, published by Pocket Books, New York.

…Moses said to the Israelites, "The Lord…has filled him with the Spirit of God, with skill, ability and knowledge in all kinds of crafts…to make artistic designs…He has filled them with skill to do all kinds of work as craftsmen, designers, embroiderers…to do the work just as the Lord has commanded."

Exodus 35:31–35

…and everyone who calls on the name of the Lord will be saved; for on Mt. Zion and in Jerusalem there will be deliverance, as the Lord has said, among the survivors whom the Lord calls.

Joel 2:32
Acts 2:21

YOU CAN'T SEE IT! You can't touch it! You can't smell it! So begins a children's game—and so began this book.

It all started with an idea to write a book about weddings as a result of a joyous family celebration. Next came the idea to self-publish, followed by a new business venture. Alongside the idea of a book on weddings, a plan had been developing to enlarge a collection of meditations written the previous year by members of a church congregation.

Did God intend for these ideas to remain just dreams, or were they visions that we would actually see, touch and smell? "In The Spirit" is, yes, a presumptuous claim, but that is what happened. We began to see, to touch, and to smell.

Women of the congregation had been earnestly making Chrismons*, which are Christmas ornaments with spiritual meanings. A child asked, "Are we in a jewelry store?" for he could see the beauty of the monograms of Christ. Each has a specific meaning. Watch for them throughout the book and see them on the tree of New Hope.

Every book needs a cover. A scented green bough, symbolizing eternal life through Jesus Christ, was cut from the cedar tree on the church property, and a beautiful Crismon, Christ's crown, was placed upon it. Next came the fragrant rose, to remind us of His beauty. The background would be wedding dress fabric left from the daughter's wedding to remind us of beginnings—the marriage covenant and our union with Christ.

Dare we go on? It was no longer just a game. We had pictures of what the cover might look like. They were given to a creative designer, who promised a cover.

Days were filled with writing letters, telling people about this new venture and asking them to be a part, to express their faith by writing, composing and designing. Now we were accountable, there was no turning back.

As publication day approached, God continued to lead to new and unexpected resources, serendipities of joy and encouragement.

IN THE SPIRIT, we have dreamed dreams and seen visions. We have smelled the roses and the cedar.

IN THE SPIRIT, we have written, composed and designed.

IN THE SPIRIT OF CHRISTMAS, which is LOVE, we offer this gift to you to join us—to see, to touch and to smell the beauty of Christ. Please accept the gift.

*From *Chrismons*, the Evangelical Lutheran Church of the Ascension, Danville, Virginia 24541 copyright 1970.

"But whoever lives by the truth comes into the light, so that it may be seen plainly that what he has done has been done through God."

–Jesus
John 3:21

"Be careful what you say to mother; it may end up in the book."

–A daughter

A man should hear a little music, read a little poetry, and see a fine picture every day of his life, in order that worldly cares may not obliterate the sense of the beautiful which God has implanted in the human soul.

–Johann Wadsworth von Goethe

"The Presence of God in Us"

Our hearts are filled with gratitude as we think of the many people who encouraged, prayed and contributed their gifts, time and other resources toward the development of this first project of Legacy House.

We reflect with wonder at our parents' careful plans and dreams for our lives. We thank God daily for our husbands and children who surrendered precious moments so this book could be completed.

The original plan for this book came from the 1986 Advent Devotional written by New Hope Community Church members, compiled and edited by Mildred Sturgeon. Her courage, talents and joyous nature have been an inspiration and blessing to all who know her.

We will both be forever grateful for the assistance of Pastor Philip Assink, Steve Allison, the Consistory and other Church members. Pastor Phil's vision of God in all areas of our lives and his guidance to live as people of integrity and destiny led us to pursue this vision.

The beauty and love of Jesus reflected in the lives and on the faces of all these people has touched us daily. We praise God, for He alone is worthy to be praised.

Beverly Stroebel
Lorraine Wilkinson

TABLE OF CONTENTS

Foreword

AS YOU READ…

It is thought that a book of devotions should have a beginning but no ending. Pages may end, but continuing devotion to our God is a precious gift that He has presented to us for the taking.

Some of the many people who have accepted the gift have recorded their thoughts in this book for you. Read one and reflect…then read another…and reflect again.

Absorb these printed thoughts realizing that God is the author speaking through His people. In that light you, too, may be inspired to "author" your own devotions to Him.

READ ON…

Dear Lord,

Thank You for bringing us together again at this time of giving thanks for Your many blessings; for a land of abundant harvests and provisions for our health and happiness; for an abundance of freedom and opportunity. We pray, Lord, that in the numerous choices we enjoy, You will lead us in the path You want us to follow, and that we will trust Your guidance, come what may, to serve Your purposes.

Thank You, Lord, for sharing this dinner with us, and we ask Your presence here as we enjoy it. In Jesus' Name.

Amen.

GIVING THANKS

A Daily Appointment With God

A FEW YEARS AGO, our pastor challenged the congregation to see how much quality time we gave to God in praise and thanks each day. He explained the benefits of having a special time and place to meet with God…in other words, an appointment with God!

Well, of the whole 24-hour day, I was feeling good about giving God, who has given me my all, from three to five minutes a day, unless I had a special task I wanted Him to perform. In a special situation, I would allow an extra five or six minutes, most of which was in seeking help from God. Needless to say, I began to have some doubts about our relationship since it appeared that most of my requests were answered, "No!"

Then one day, it came to me to heed the teachings that I learned many years ago, the words I had said as a young child. Those words were Bible verses that were taught to every child in Sunday school. The striking opening of each verse suddenly came to me: "In the beginning God!" and "In the beginning was the Word!"

Well, I tried it. I made a commitment to God, to God and no one else! I would find a secret and private place, would talk to God with praise and thanksgiving, and I would do this the very first thing each morning. I put my new commitment into action. Before talking with anyone else, I would go with God—in the bathroom. Believe me, you can't find a place more private than the bathroom!

But each day I was distracted and challenged, one day by the dog, another day by the telephone, or still another day by my family. I knew that Satan was trying to come between me and my appointment with God; he caused me to be distracted and late each morning. In fact, it became so bad that it occurred to me that if I were on a job with this kind of performance, I would be fired. If I were traveling, I would be left behind. Yet still, my God was patient with me.

Then one day as I was doing a Bible study, I read that Satan is strong, but God is stronger. In another scripture of the same lesson I read that God makes us willing to do His will. Now this was not the first time I had read either verse, but what was unique is that this was the first time that it seemed that God was talking to me.

Well, that was then. Now, each morning I really keep my appointment with God. The telephone seldom rings, and if it does, I ignore it. My family now has more respect for my right to privacy in the early morning. Even the dog will lay quietly outside the door until I exit the bathroom! Thus, Satan has lost, and through God's power and strength, I now keep my appointment with God, and I talk to Him with praise and thanksgiving each morning. This all started on that precious day that I remembered the striking opening of those Bible verses: Genesis 1:1 "In the beginning God!" and John 1:1 "In the beginning was the Word!"

If only we, the descendants of God's creation, would put God in the beginning of our day! Just think of how uplifting it would be to start each day with praise, adoration, and submission to God and His will! If you have not yet made this commitment, this season is a beautiful time to start, a season that starts with Thanksgiving, and lasts until after Christmas.

To give thanks for all the things we are thankful for calls for some reflection on our part: reflection on our ancestors, and their experiences and hardships, and how much easier it is for us; reflection on the peoples of some other nations, their plight, their hunger, and their uprooting and pestilence resulting from continuous and constant warfare, and how much more tranquil it is for us; reflection on those countries under the self-imposed rule of dictatorships that torment, torture and suppress the will and well-being of the people, while we enjoy the freedom of self expression as well as the power to elect or even cast out our leaders; reflection on your healthy left arm in spite of the loss of the right arm; reflection on your good vision in spite of the fact that your ears do not hear and your lips cannot speak; reflection on how well you can walk in spite of the fact that your eyes cannot see; and reflection on the knowledge that when things are not going well for the moment, we can have hope for the future!

But we must not use these reflections to boast of our status or our blessings; rather we simply reflect to help us understand that when we go to our secret and private place for our daily appointment with God, we should not be quick to ask for favors or special requests. He has already provided and continues to provide. Thus, our reflecting causes us to talk to God with praise, with adoration and with thanksgiving. Failure to reflect can cause us to feel rejected and despondent... very much alone.

When you are diseased, find consolation in thinking of Job or the leper. When friends and family turn against you, reflect on David and how long Saul sought to destroy him. And if you are the vilest of all sinners, think of the forgiven criminal who was crucified with Jesus.

If you take the time to reflect each day, then you will truly be most thankful. As Christmas approaches, then you will really be able to understand what the poet was feeling when he wrote, "How Great Thou Art," and then we can celebrate the birth of Jesus with shouts of joy and praise, and, "Hallelujah!", of thanksgiving!

I bid you peace, I give you my love, and I offer you this challenge to find your own secret and private place. Then start each day with A DAILY APPOINTMENT WITH GOD!"

A Spiritual Legacy Of Ours

ONE OF THE SPIRITUAL LEGACIES we have as Americans is relatively unknown to us. How many of us know of the writing of Christopher Columbus' personal faith in God? The following document from his BOOK OF PROPHECIES is published only in Spanish.

"It was the Lord who put into my mind (I could feel his hand upon me) the fact that it would be possible to sail from here to the Indies. All who heard of my project rejected it with laughter, ridiculing me. There is no question that the inspiration was from the Holy Spirit, because He comforted me with rays of marvelous inspiration from the Holy Scripture.

"I am a most unworthy sinner, but I have cried out to the Lord for grace and mercy and they have covered me completely. I have found the sweetest consolation since I make it my whole purpose to enjoy His marvelous presence. For the execution of the journey to the Indies, I did not make use of intelligence, mathematics or maps. It is simply the fulfillment of what Isaiah prophesied.

"No one should fear to undertake any task in the name of our Saviour, if it is just and if the intention is purely for His holy service. The working out of all things has been assigned to each person by our Lord, but it all happens according to His sovereign will, even though He gives advice. He lacks nothing that it is in the power of men to give Him. Oh, what a gracious Lord, who desires that people should perform for Him those things for which He holds Himself responsible! Day and night, moment by moment, everyone should express their most devoted gratitude to Him."

Corporate Prayer

In this same spirit, let us begin our Thanksgiving season by acknowledging with gratitude our great legacy from those that have gone before us.

Almighty God, Lord of creation, Father of all nations:

WE, THE PEOPLE, praise You for establishing our nation. We celebrate with gratitude those explorers who risked everything because they trusted in You. Help us to trust wholly in you.

WE, THE PEOPLE, praise You for our founding ancestors. In their efforts to establish a new nation, You guided them to provide space for worship, for justice, and for freedom. May we be guided by Your Spirit to sustain these great gifts.

WE, THE PEOPLE, give thanks for those who have sacrificed for freedom. Many have had to fight, some even die, to maintain this free land. Others have taken courageous stands to correct injustice and enhance this free land. May we be willing to sacrifice to sustain this heritage.

WE, THE PEOPLE, give thanks for the abundance of this land. Not only is food sent from our "bread basket" to every corner of the world, but also creative minds have contributed to the physical and medical needs of our world. Help us, O God, to use and to invest our resources wisely.

WE, THE PEOPLE, give thanks for those who have persevered in the proclamation of Your Word. Through seasons of great awakening and valleys of spiritual decay, faithful servants have gone about the task of bearing witness to Your saving grace. May we with grateful and determined hearts continue to announce the good news.

> *"Since we are surrounded by such a great cloud of witnesses, let us throw off everything that hinders and the sin that so easily entangles, and let us run with perseverance the race marked out for us. Let us fix our eyes on Jesus, the author and perfector of our faith, who for the joy set before him endured the cross, scorning its shame, and sat down at the right hand of the throne of God."*
> Amen.

Hebrews 12: 1, 2

For the Founding Fathers

WE THE PEOPLE of the United States, in order to form a more perfect Union, establish justice, insure domestic tranquility, provide for the common defense, promote the general welfare, and secure the blessings of liberty to ourselves and our posterity, do ordain and establish this Constitution for the United States of America.

Preamble of the United States Constitution

FROM MAY 25 TO SEPTEMBER 17, 1787, a federal convention of the thirteen colonies was held in Philadelphia. The stated purpose of the meeting was to revise or change the Articles of Confederation, the existing loose-knit form of central government. Instead, the fifty-five delegates who attended drew up a document which has proven to be the most successful working constitution in the history of the world. William E. Gladstone, ex-Prime Minister of England, referred to it as the greatest work ever produced by the minds of men. It is amazing that a Constitution written two hundred years ago for thirteen colonies or states remains viable today for fifty states and continues to affect our daily lives more than any other written work.

Of course, the Constitution was a civil document rather than a religious one and it is difficult to say with any accuracy how many of the Founding Fathers were practicing Christians. Yet, it is apparent that they had certain expectations: that the document they wrote would be used by people whose ideas about government included a dependence on the sovereignty of God and ethics and morality based on Biblical standards and respect for the individual.

One of the greatest concerns of the writers of the Constitution and the Bill of Rights, which was added shortly after the Constitution was ratified, was the wide diversity of religious traditions amongst its members. Putting aside doctrinal differences, they established a system whereby religion could but did not necessarily play a role in each person's life.

Three of the most influential members of the Convention were George Washington, Benjamin Franklin, and James Monroe. These three leaders showed their belief in the necessity for Divine leadership if their work was to be successful and in the important role that religion would play in the nation's history.

"It is impossible to account for the creation of the universe, without the agency of a Supreme Being. It is impossible to govern the universe, without the aid of a Supreme Being. It is impossible to reason without arriving at a Supreme Being. If there had been no God, mankind would have been obliged to imagine one.

—George Washington

Referring to the Declaration of Independence, John Adams wrote:

"Yesterday the greatest question was decided which ever was debated in America; and a greater perhaps never was, nor will be, decided among men. A resolution was passed without one dissenting colony, that these United Colonies are, and of right ought to be, free and independent States."

Letter to Abigail Adams, 3 July 1776

The great French historian Alexis de Tocqueville wrote, speaking of the American people as a whole:

I do not know whether all Americans have a sincere faith in their religion— for who can search the human heart—but I am certain that they hold it to be indispensable to the maintenance of republican institutions.

—Alexis de Tocqueville

God's Gift

Did you ever trust God's promises
When you bowed in prayer?
Did you expect an answer?
Did you leave your troubles there?

If you believed upon His Word,
Then you found sweet release.
A joy and trust not known before,
A deep, abiding peace.

The gift of God to troubled hearts
Is free to all His own.
The world is brighter for His love.
We never walk alone.

Lois Watts

George Washington, Virginia planter and chairman of the convention, was a member of the Episcopal Church. When the delegates first assembled, and a heated discussion developed over the issue of whether they should revise the Articles or write a new Constitution, he summarized his thoughts by saying that "It is probable that no plan we propose will be adopted. Let us raise a standard to which the wise and honest can repair. The event is in the hands of God."

Benjamin Franklin, at eighty-one years of age the most venerated and honored of the delegates, proved to be a tremendous influence for compromise. At a critical time in the proceedings, Franklin, never known as a man of strong faith in Christ, acknowledged God's role in the work of the delegates in a speech in which he said:

> "In the beginning of the contest with Britain, when we were sensible of danger, we had daily prayers in this room for Divine protection. Our prayers…were heard and were graciously answered. And have we now forgotten this powerful Friend? Or do we imagine we no longer need His assistance? I have lived a long time, and the longer I live, the more convincing proofs I see of this truth: 'that God governs in the affairs of man.' And if a sparrow cannot fall to the ground without His notice, is it probable that an empire can rise without His aid?"

James Madison, an influential delegate from Virginia, later became the fourth president of the United States. When a young man, Madison attended the College of New Jersey (now Princeton University), where he studied Hebrew, ethics, history, and theology. His tutor at the college was John Witherspoon, the highly respected Presbyterian clergyman, scholar, and statesman. One of Madison's major concerns was freedom of religion, or the right of all people to worship God as they so desired. As a member of the delegation to draw up a constitution for Virginia in 1776, he moved successfully for the inclusion of a clause for the free exercise of religion. When the Bill of Rights was added to the U.S. Constitution in 1790, Madison was primarily responsible for the free exercise of religion clause in the first amendment.

Under the Constitution, rights and prohibitions are not inviolable. They are subject to interpretation and applied by politically chosen authorities. As citizens, we enjoy a remarkable amount of liberty. Government has a God-given task to preserve justice. In order to preserve justice in our system of open political processes, we have a responsibility to constantly be determined and willing to pursue righteousness.

Thanksgiving–Commitment or Complacency?

THANKSGIVING IS A TIME TO THANK our Heavenly Father for giving us the "Land of the Free and the Home of the Brave." Despite constant danger, our heritage has been one of commitment to freedom and bravery, starting with our forefathers who, under God's guidance formed this great nation. Since then, national leaders have been and are committed to maintain our freedom. That commitment also has been and is found in many young people who have fought in several wars, including two World Wars, Korea and Vietnam. For some, the commitment has been fatal, for they died in the service of their country; and even though we are at peace today, many young people are dedicating themselves to the service of our country. We pray to God that this commitment will not demand the supreme sacrifice, and that peace will be our future.

However, that future will not be secure unless we have commitment rather than complacency. We must exercise our hard-fought right to vote, select our leaders and support our service personnel. We must encourage and pray for them. We cannot be complacent about our future. In the past, draft card and flag burners were on the news. Today, the "me, first" generation concerns many thoughtful citizens. Both generations are a threat to commitment and an invitation to complacency. We must not let that happen!

What a privilege to live in the United States! Thanks be to God for allowing our nation to remain free, and giving us brave leaders and servicemen and servicewomen.

Thanksgiving Prayer: "…that we may then all unite in rendering unto Him our sincere and humble thanks for His kind care and protection of the people of this country, previous to their becoming a nation; for the signal manifold mercies, and the favorable interpositions of His providence, in the course and conclusion of the late war; for the great degree of tranquillity, union and plenty which we have enjoyed; for the peaceable and rational manner in which we have been enabled to establish Constitutions of Government for our safety and happiness, and particularly the national one now lately instituted; for the civil and religious liberty with which we are blessed, and the means we have of acquiring and diffusing useful knowledge; and, in general, for all the great and various favors, which He has been pleased to confer upon us."* Amen.

Applying Our Thanks: Pray, that the words of an early World War II song may ever be true: "…that rain and snow may be all that fall from the skies above."

*First Thanksgiving Proclamation–President George Washington–1789

"Blessed is the nation whose God is the Lord, the people he chose for his inheritance."

Psalm 37:5

"For to us a child is born, to us a son is given, and the government will be on his shoulders. And he will be called Wonderful Counselor, Mighty God, Everlasting Father, Prince of Peace."

Isaiah 9:6

"With this high honor devolves upon you also a corresponding responsibility. As the country herein trusts you, so under God, it will sustain you. I scarcely need add, that with what I here speak for the nation goes my own hearty personal concurrence."

Abraham Lincoln–upon the commissioning of General Ulysses S. Grant

A Scenario of Faith...In Three Scenes

The River

I am the river,
The swirling, silver white
water
always moving...
At times
to touch the earth
until, as always,
I am dragged away
Never to smell the rose...
Only a quick glimpse
before, once again,
I am whisked away.
There a deer,
and a squirrel,
an old 'coon and a shaggy bear,
two lovers walking...
together
under a starlit sky.
Oh, what I would give
to join in life
Once,
just once,
to be a part of love.
But, as always,
I am the river
always moving
and yet,
never touched.

Scott M. Manly

Scene 1:

A bright August morning, my fifty-seventh birthday. A knock at the door, a man in blue, only key words grasped in his solemn message:

YOUR SON...SCOTT...KILLED ... LIGHTNING... PHILMONT...DETAILS FOLLOW.

Shock...a sense of loneliness...disbelief supplanted almost immediately by a bond and obligation to the living...wife and daughter equally numbed and grasping for...and finding...faith in kinship and love.

Scene 2:

Outpourings of respect and honor for the son who lives...but now in memories of intimate relationships with family and close friends...and flashing vignettes of others whose paths crossed Scott's only briefly but are remembered...with vibrancy and appreciation. Church support that is the stuff of which sermons are created, delivered, and, most importantly, lived. Faith that not only sustains, but uplifts.

Scene 3:

Flag-draped casket, military escort, taps, a fly-by all bearing testimony to Scott's tie to "his" academy, his country, his allegiances. A father, proudly and firmly, says his good-byes on behalf of others whose hearts must say what their mouths cannot.

During the years Scott spent at the Air Force Academy, it was my daily practice to sit at my office typewriter and compose a letter to him. I would share with you my final letter to Scott, written yesterday, hoping that it might prove as reassuring to you as it proved reassuring and uplifting to my spirits writing it:

Dear Scott...

The temptation this morning, my son, is to pour out my grief at the suddenness of your death and the subsequent brevity of your life, but I find that more necessary for me is to draw upon my memories and my faith and dwell instead on the quality of that life, and celebrate the boy you were, the man you are, and praise God for loaning you to all of us who loved and respected the qualities you developed and utilized so fully. In that light, I remember:

There was deep stillness in the hospital ward as there had been stillness on the field of Gettysburg. The soldier's voice broke it. "It's a wonderful speech," he said. "There's nothing finer. Other men have spoken stirring words, for the North and for the South, but never before, I think, with the love of both breathing through them…. To feel that your enemy can fight you to death without malice, with charity—it lifts country, it lifts humanity to something worth dying for."
—Excerpt from "The Perfect Tribute," a story containing the Gettysburg Address by Mary R.S. Andrews

Scott the Boy Scout

who, in his teens, recited the Boy Scout Law and then spent the rest of his years on earth living it to the letter of its intent and design;

Scott the Student

who challenged his teachers with his keen, probing mind and then rewarded them by assimilating and applying what they had taught to hone still more sharply the intellectual powers that had been God-given. In accordance with a motto on the grounds of the U.S. Air Force Academy which states, "Man's flight through life is sustained by the power of his knowledge," Scott was more than sustained…he was inspired;

Scott, the Athlete

who took his Grandfather MacVean's philosophy of coaching, "Play the sport with honesty and integrity" and broadened it to include every component of physical endeavor on the playground of life.

Scott, the Teacher

who, though he will never attain his aspiration to teach at the Air Force Academy, was teaching right up to the final moment of his life in the most important ways: by precept and example;

Scott, the Creative Artist

who took his Grandfather Manly's talent with words and transformed simple words into beautiful thoughts on life like those expressed in his poem, *The River;*

Scott, the Patriot

whose love for America was significantly "signed, sealed and delivered" the day he committed himself to a life of service to his country in the Air Force and to the flag that now, symbolically, is draped across his casket;

Scott, the Academy Cadet

who successfully proved to his superiors and to himself his ability to "beast it out" through his doolie year and proceed, with ever-increasing enthusiasm, pride, and accomplishment to his final, and best designation as a cadet: FIRST CLASS;

<u>Scott, the Friend</u>

who was ever known as consistent and true, perceptive and positive, and supportive in the way one expects of truly good friends;

and finally,

<u>Scott, the nephew, cousin, grandson, son, and brother</u>

who enriched and ennobled our lives by the full measure of his caring and sharing of his many successes and his failures (all of which escape my remembrance just now). He seemed to give so much more than he received–giving because he wanted to, not because he expected something in return.

I could go on, but emotions overwhelm me. But, Scott, in closing, I would share an incident which occurred to me this morning that seemed to be God's way of speaking directly to me and reassuring me that all is right, despite my heavy heart. It was just before dawn, and I had gone out to pick up the morning newspaper. I happened to look up to the sky, and there I saw a single star, surely the brightest star I have ever seen in my life. You, Scott, probably could have identified it by its scientific name, but I simply now think of it as SCOTT'S STAR–symbolizing you, no longer earth-bound and fettered by mortal limitations, but now moving onward and upward in keeping with your God-given abilities in spheres that are beyond the ken of human comprehension. That thought sustains and uplifts me as I say, "God speed, my son."

I close, as ever, with Kathleen's, your mother's, and my everlasting love–always and all ways.

DAD

Prayer:

<u>Lord, Guard and Guide the Men Who Fly</u>

Lord, Guard and Guide the men who fly
Through the great Spaces of the Sky;
Be with them traversing the air
In darkening storms or sunshine fair.

Amen
(Mary C.D. Hamilton)

The Influence of the Holy

Do not laugh
when I say
the stars have spoken.

If you
have never listened,
why what token
would you, could you
know them?

Some words they send,
some dreams they stir
are two-edged,
blue-edged swords
which cut between
the moments
to spaces there,
where time
takes no measure—
there in
that second mirage
where our dreams
and spiritualities
lodge.

(A mirage—
a something-wandered
from another sphere
is lost
in this most literal
here.

And our dreams—
when thundering
and riding horseback,
do those of the day
carry any less fright
than those
of the night?

Or when they
flow with golden promise,
do those of the night
seem any less sweet
than those
the sunbursts greet?)

The stars have spoken.
Did you listen
with your spirits?
Or did you
laugh as at a mirage
and say
you didn't hear it?

If we hide
long enough,
playing solitaire,
someday,
when we look,
will we find
nobody there?

Just a first mirage
played against
a shadow land,
over shallows spanned?

Heed the stars:
they are
ever bright
though oft
we do not see them
or hear their cries.

For it is written:
Great men
are not always wise;
neither do the aged
understand judgement.

Do not come
to judgement barren
with a child's
first conception.

If days can speak
or stored up years,
who should say
stars are the exception?

And it aught
is written in the stars,
which then, in season,
speak,
Oh, my God,
there is
an awesome reason.

Mavis Christensen

Lord, Guard and Guide the Men Who Fly

2. You who support with tender might
The balanced birds in all their flight,
Lord of the tempered winds, be near,
That, having you, they know no fear.

3. Control their minds with instinct fit
Whene'er, adventuring, they quit
The firm security of land;
Grant steadfast eye and skillful hand.

4. Aloft in solitudes of space,
Uphold them with your saving grace.
O God, protect the men who fly
Through lonely ways beneath the sky. Amen.

The Beautiful Place

Oh, the beauty of this place.
Of one, lone star in all the
vastnesses of space,
As evening falls.

Of stark, black branches,
In fretwork of design
Against the cold, clearness
Of a winter sky.

Such loveliness as I can see
From my own window
Fair puts to shame all doubts
And scorning of eternal love.

Who but a Spirit tender and compassionate
Could lift my spirit from its earthly habitat
To highest pinnacle of heaven
By one lone star
And stark black branches
Against a winter sky?

Lois Watts

Friends in Christ

Friends in Christ, what sweeter way
To draw us closer day by day.
No fellowship on earth more sweet,
Together at the Saviour's feet.
His love supreme, yes, that is sure—
To love you no less, but love Him more.

                                   Lois Watts

Lessons Learned In Our Marriage Through Family

There are different kinds of gifts, but the same Spirit. There are different kinds of service, but the same Lord. There are different kinds of working, but the same God works all of them in all men.

Now to each one the manifestation of the Spirit is given for the common good. To one there is given through the Spirit the message of wisdom, to another the message of knowledge by means of the same Spirit, to another faith by the same Spirit, to another gifts of healing by that one Spirit, to another miraculous powers, to another prophecy, to another distinguishing between spirits, to another speaking in different kinds of tongues, and to still another the interpretation of tongues. All these are the work of one and the same Spirit, and he gives them to each one, just as he determines.

I Corinthians 12: 4–11

THIS HAS BEEN A WONDERFUL SUMMER for us—wonderful because we could spend parts of it with our children and grandchildren.

Late in April we left for England (a perfect time to visit England before all the tourists arrive and when it is green and the flowers are a riot of color). We came to spend time with our older son and his family. Barbara and Dave have three boys who had grown up since we saw them last. Dave was on a year's sabbatical leave from his university and had returned to Sheffield to continue his study of the people and culture of that area as an urban anthropologist. There we went sightseeing, visiting, hiking, and reacquainting ourselves with our "English" family.

Then later in July we drove from California to Michigan to the cottage for wonderful relaxing times with our son Rick, his wife, and their three beautiful girls. Rick is an apprentice Golf Course Superintendent, so with golfing, fishing, eating, and visiting; it was a great time.

We were also able to spend time there and later in Louisville, Kentucky, with Mary and John and their two children, where we learned more of what it means to head a great seminary and lead a campaign to get the Presbyterians to move their headquarters to Louisville.

What a wonder each family is—each with its own special gifts. Our scripture passage deals with spiritual gifts. The love that radiates through each family has to originate in a spiritual love. The commitment to service of our Lord and His church is a spiritual gift as well, proven by how the marriages have survived and grown.

To see each family working, worshipping, and living out their lives with such joy makes our lives full. What a wonderful way to look forward to a real Thanksgiving!

Prayer: Thank You, Father, for our families. Our lives are full of their love. Amen.

Applying Our Thanks: God's gifts are life leading and life changing!

Lessons Learned In Our Marriage Through Service

"Be strong and courageous, because you will lead these people to inherit the land I swore to their forefathers to give them. Be strong and very courageous. Be careful to obey all the law my servant Moses gave you; do not turn from it to the right or to the left, that you may be successful wherever you go. Do not let this Book of the Law depart from your mouth; meditate on it day and night, so that you may be careful to do everything written in it. Then you will be prosperous and successful. Have I not commanded you? Be strong and courageous. Do not be terrified; do not be discouraged, for the Lord your God will be with you wherever you go."

Joshua 1: 6–9

Early in our marriage we learned some lessons that have given us equanimity on our road through life in a variety of circumstances.

After being married on September 8, 1942, and being assured that Harry would go overseas, we were delighted to learn that I could join him in Corpus Christi, Texas, at Thanksgiving time. After one month we left for Fort Worth, Texas. Soon we went by train to Jacksonville, Florida, on to Sanford, Florida and to Key West. Harry went overseas then for eleven months and I went back to Michigan to have a baby–Mary Margaret. Then in July of '44, back to Key West, on to the Eastern shore of Maryland, to Atlanta, Georgia, to San Francisco, and of all places to Baldwin, Kansas.

What did we learn from all these moves and living in all these places? We learned to accept what the Lord has given us and call it adventure.

We found that if we put forth an effort, we could find wonderful Christian friends and share worship experiences in stimulating churches wherever we were. We went to Presbyterian churches, Methodist, even a Methodist Episcopal, a Christian Church, Baptist, and more. When Mary was with us we found nurseries and young people like ourselves.

In 1983 we shared a reunion with members of Harry's Navy pilots' Squadron V P 143 in South Padre Island, Texas. We joined about fifteen couples who had experienced many of those moves with us in W W II during those scarey years. To our amazement and delight we found that all of these people were in one way or another involved in church work in many kinds of endeavors from Presbyterian Women's Work on a high level to work in a Catholic Boys' Home, to A. A. We had chosen the right friends back in '42–'44 and always since seemed to find Christian friends wherever God placed us.

In retirement we are blessed to have found work in our church. We are actively serving on several charity boards and are busy tutoring foreign students to read and write in English.

The Lord knows where to put us to work and we are thankful He has found places for us to serve.

Prayer: Our Father, give us the courage to order our steps that our walk toward our destination will always be close to You. Amen.

Applying Our Thanks: The Lord is with you wherever you go.

God is our refuge and strength, an ever-
  present help in trouble.
Therefore we will not fear, though the
  earth give way
  and the mountains fall into the heart of
  the sea,
though its waters roar and foam
  and the mountains quake with their
  surging.

There is a river whose streams make glad
  the city of God,
  the holy place where the Most High
  dwells.
God is within her, she will not fall;
  God will help her at break of day.
Nations are in uproar, kingdoms fall;
  he lifts his voice, the earth melts.

The Lord Almighty is with us;
  the God of Jacob is our fortress.

Come and see the works of the Lord,
  the desolations he has brought on the
  earth.
He makes wars cease to the ends of the
  earth;
  he breaks the bow and shatters the
  spear,
  he burns the shields with fire.
"Be still, and know that I am God;
  I will be exalted among the nations,
  I will be exalted in the earth."

The Lord Almighty is with us;
  the God of Jacob is our fortress.
                              Psalm 46

Can You Fix It?

THE TOUCH OF TYPEWRITER KEYS beneath busy fingers worked its usual magic—the thrill of writing a first novel; wonderful expectations, however naive—the sheer audacity and yet utter joy of daring to approach even the most outward perimeter of the very fount of creativity—more than sufficient to wipe away the rigors of an already fourteen hour day; Air Force commander become author, peasant turned expectant poet, day to day things of a mundane world metamorphosed into indescribable ecstasy. And then, sweet Jesus, it happened! It was like a bolt of satanic thunder expelled from the deepest depths of hell—a zillion bolts of terror—a sledge hammer of unbearable pain propelled by the hand of some yet unknown but soon to become familiar herculian monster crashed about lower neck and shoulders teaching its horrible lesson—the meaning of pain. But it was not to be long endured. God granted the blessing of unconsciousness, and I awoke hours later with my face nestled in the carriage of my suddenly silenced typewriter.

There was no need for medical assistance—the pain was gone as mysteriously as it had come. The next day was busy with briefing Generals, and then came the long awaited balm of a soft warm bed, the sweetness of an angel wife, and, at last, sleep. Oh, God, not again!! Pain like lightning born in a tormented brain exploded through anguished nerves and screamed forth in a rush for release from tortured fingers and toes. Four flight surgeons huddled in a corner tried not to be overheard by the stricken but interesting "neuro-case" writhing on their examining table. "Tell me, damn it! I've got a right to know! What's wrong with me!" Wish I had not asked.

"Something compressing your spinal cord."

"Oh really, like what?"

"Probably a tumor!"

"Oh, God, could it be cancer?"

"Most likely!"

"Operable?"

"Probably not."

My reaction was more than simple denial or some self induced comforting delusion. There was not even the slightest hint of wishful thinking. No matter what these well intentioned jerks were telling me, I was not going to die—at least not quite yet. God loved me, and He told me so, and that was all there was to it. Call it what you will. Most would call it faith. For me then, and now, it was the joy of His presence suddenly filling my heart.

But now, this is what the Lord says—

he who created you, O Jacob,
he who formed you, O Israel:
"Fear not, for I have redeemed you;
I have summoned you by name; you are mine.

When you pass through the waters, I will be with you;
and when you pass through the rivers, they will not sweep over you.
When you walk through the fire, you will not be burned;
the flames will not set you ablaze.

For I am the Lord, your God, the Holy One of Israel, your Savior;
I give Egypt for your ransom, Cush and Seba in your stead.

Isaiah 43: 1–3

To some, God gave the gift of healing. To Thomas E. Carter, M.D. neurosurgeon, He gave this gift abundantly, then filled him to overflowing with other gifts of love, compassion, understanding and concern.

Tom told it like it was. "The good news is there is no tumor. The bad news is you've got a calcified disc compressing your cervical spine."

"Can you fix it?"

"Maybe, but it's very risky. I'll have to use experimental techniques. The odds for a favorable outcome aren't good."

"Like what's a favorable outcome?"

"Waking up when it's over—or quadraplegia, or optimistically paraplegia."

"You mean there's *no* chance I'll walk away from this?"

"Not much of one, but you might!"

There it was again, loud and clear, the tender touch of God's loving hand on my shoulder, a rush of joy filling my being. "I'll be fine, Doctor. When do we get started?"

They sent me the Catholic chaplain by mistake the evening before surgery. I did not tell him I was a protestant until he had finished praying for me. I did not want to miss any possible help; but I told him and the protestant chaplain, who came later, how I felt about God's involvement in all this. The protestant chaplain must have been moved—he preached about it the next Sunday.

From the vantage point of looking up from the table at Tom's beautiful black face framed in green scrubs I saw it all—healer, scientist, dispenser of miracles. Then I saw the scalpel just as consciousness faded.

Buttercups. Unbelievably beautiful. Intensely yellow. Heavenly choirs, music from the lips of angels. A joy of such intense loveliness, I could not bear the thought of ever leaving. But, of course, I had to leave, to come back at least for an unknown time; but I already knew, because God had made it clear He had other things for me to do.

The same beautiful green surrounded black faced saint became my one-more-found earthly reality as I blinked back into consciousness some twelve hours after all of this had begun. For some twelve hours this wonderful, gloriously gifted servant of God and man looked through his electronic microscope so he could see more clearly to pick fragments of bone from the regions of my spine.

"Move your right foot," Tom said. "Good, now your left." Then he took my right hand in his. "Wiggle your fingers," he said. Then, smiling for the first time, he said, taking my left hand, "Now move this one." I did, and he exclaimed with unabashed joy what I had known from the beginning. "You're going to be just fine, Bob."

Prayer: Praise God I was and am. Amen.

Educate Us Lord

WE WHO ARE PARENTS, teachers, or students must begin with prayer for one another that God will bless and honor those individuals specifically involved with our family's lives.

Thank you Father for being in control in all situations at all times. I praise you Lord for my teachers, my students and the parents that I will come to know. I ask you now to give me your wisdom, your love and the power of your Holy Spirit to be sensitive to their needs and of my needs as well. Honor this relationship, Lord.

In Jesus' Name, Amen

Now you are the body of Christ, and each one of you is a part of it. And in the church God has appointed first of all apostles, second prophets, third teachers, then workers of miracles, also those having gifts of healing, those able to help others, those with gifts of administration, and those speaking in different kinds of tongues.

I Corinthians 12: 27–28

The Lord God Himself will appoint many. It is a great responsibility to be a teacher.

Not many of you should presume to be teachers, my brothers, because you know that we who teach will be judged more strictly. We all stumble in many ways. If anyone is never at fault in what he says, he is a perfect man, able to keep his whole body in check..

James 3: 1–2

Be sensitive to what kind of person your teacher or student is. Get to know them if you seek to teach them or learn from them. Getting to know people and showing them that you care is one way God can minister through you and He will enable you to know and see through His eyes.

A student is not above his teacher, nor a servant above his master. It is enough for the student to be like his teacher, and the servant like his master. If the head of the house has been called Beelzebub, how much more the members of his household! So do not be afraid of them. There is nothing concealed that will not be disclosed or hidden that will not be made known.

Matthew 10: 24–26

It is at the Lord's last supper with His beloved disciples that He teaches them to serve others. He washes their feet–the humblest example He could offer them. He lowers Himself to instruct them how to reach others and how to teach.

You call me 'Teacher' and 'Lord,' and rightly so, for that is what I am.

John 13:13

Show concern and genuine caring for the student or the teacher for when we do, we know if we are given a chance to befriend an angel, a messenger of God.

Keep on loving each other as brothers. Do not forget to entertain strangers, for by so doing some people have entertained angels without knowing it.

Hebrews 13: 1–2

When there is conflict among teachers and parents and students or any other relationship, and situations seem impossible read:

Keep your lives free from the love of money and be content with what you have, because God has said,
   "Never will I leave you;
     never will I forsake you."
So we say with confidence,
   "The Lord is my helper; I will not be afraid.
    What can man do to me?"

Hebrews 13: 5–6

Be confident in the Lord's control, stand firm in the promises and know His perfect peace. Let nothing be in your home that you know is evil. Do not give Satan living room in your home. Give the seekers and learners in your home a healthy environment to develop in Christ's image, not in Satan's. Seek goodness.

My eyes have seen the defeat of my
    adversaries;
  my ears have heard the rout of my
    wicked foes.
         Psalm 92:11

Turn from evil and do good;
  seek peace and pursue it.
         Psalm 34:14

Prayer: Thank You blessed Savior for leading us to salvation and for Your holy words that You have spoken and directed in Your scripture. Thank You Jesus for life, Your very life that will always be there to instruct and show us where You would have our hearts and minds be drawing us nearer to You. That special life with You is so urgent, yet we allow our day to fill up first, leaving You last on our list many times. Forgive us, strengthen us, and teach us of the power that we too can have daily in living that confident, secure life that only You can provide.

Praise in Jesus' Name, Amen.

Applying Our Thanks: Give thanks today for a parent, a teacher or a student in your past or in your present situation, and for the Lord's continual teaching.

For Friends When I Need Them Most

GOD HAS PROMISED to supply all our needs. When I think about this promise I tend to think only of our financial and material needs. But in God's infinite wisdom, He knew we had additional needs.

As I look back over my life, I realize that God has supplied friends as one way to fill emotional and social needs. As a child He provided friends to join in bike-riding and Camp Fire Girls. In High School He provided special people on those first lonely days at a new school in a different country, friends for the bus ride, and a special friend to take me to the prom. In College there were friends to pull pranks on, to stay up all night with, and to help me pass Algebra. As I grew older God provided friends in co-workers, in-laws, sisters, parents and my husband, who is my best friend. Recently, after moving to a new town, God supplied friends who helped make the adjustment much easier.

God also supplied friends for some of the greatest people in the Bible: Ruth and Naomi; David and Jonathan; Daniel and his three friends; Paul, Priscilla and Aquila; Mary, Martha and Lazarus; and Jesus and His disciples. Ruth proved her dedication and friendship to her mother-in-law by leaving the land of her family and birth to live in a foreign land. Jonathan swore eternal friendship with David because of his deep affection for him. (I Samuel 18:3)

Prayer: Thank You, Lord, for filling our every need. Thank you for each person who has in some way enriched our lives and given us that very special gift of friendship. Please teach us to be open to accepting and giving the gift of friendship to others. Amen.

Applying Our Thanks: Does a friend of yours need a word of encouragement? Write a note today.

**Within the Circus Maximus
to the back shop
at The Daily Intelligencer**

*I pass from family to family
and from friend to friend
in a progression
which has no end.*

*We are circles winding 'round
in a never-ending spiral;
we give each other love
through happy times and trial.*

*You have been my friend
and become my family;
brothers, sisters have we been,
a jolly homily.*

*I will treasure all
the joyous memory
of what you've been and given,
and leave a thought with thee:*

*If you can't love
those you hold so dear,
then by all means, in all ways,
love the ones you're near.*

Mavis Christensen

Always giving thanks to God the Father for everything, in the name of our Lord Jesus Christ.

Ephesians 5: 20

Finally, be strong in the Lord and in his mighty power. Put on the full armor of God so that you can take your stand against the devil's schemes. For our struggle is not against flesh and blood, but against the rulers, against the authorities, against the powers of this dark world and against the spiritual forces of evil in the heavenly realms. Therefore put on the full armor of God, so that when the day of evil comes, you may be able to stand your ground, and after you have done everything, to stand. Stand firm then with the belt of truth buckled around your waist, with the breastplate of righteousness in place, and with your feet fitted with the readiness that comes from the gospel of peace. In addition to all this, take up the shield of faith, with which you can extinguish all the flaming arrows of the evil one. Take the helmet of salvation and the sword of the Spirit, which is the word of God.

Ephesians 6: 10–17

…Thanks A Lot!…

PAUL INSTRUCTS US TO THANK GOD for all things. How can we really do that? A paycheck that bounces or an act of carelessness that causes a major disaster do not seem like things for which we should be thankful, do they? How can we be thankful when our loving God allows great pain to come to us? Why does Paul give us this seemingly masochistic order?

Reading on in this letter to the Ephesians, beginning at verse 10, we discover the real meat of this teaching. Our thanks is not to be for the thing, but for the knowledge that God's power and God's resources are boundless!

This, then, is the real truth: God is our provider; not an employer's bank account, or any human being, or any worldly thing. God. When we internalize this fact, we can remove that which impedes our ability to respond with true thankfulness to this loving God.

Prayer: Loving heavenly Father, in the Name of our Lord Jesus Christ, please accept our praise and our thanks for being so utterly dependable. Amen.

Applying Our Thanks: The Dutch say:
"Wat leven wij toch gelukkig."
meaning "We are so lucky to be living this way "

Fill Me With Thy Grace

Dmi   Gmi   Cmi   F13
mit my-self a- new,   I   draw up- on Thy   strength and, Lord, I
Bbmaj7 Cmi7   Bbmaj9 Bb13   Eb   F/Eb
claim new life from   You.   I de-   pend up- on Your   guid- ance for with-
RIT.
A TEMPO
Bb/D   Cmi   Bb   Eb (SLOWER)   Bb/F   Gmi
out it I would   stray,   Lord just as a child I   come to You and
Cmi7   F13   Bb9   Bb   Fmi7(b5)   Eb   Cmi   Cmi7
RIT.
bold-ly I can   pray: Je- sus, yes, on-ly   Je- sus,   Your
D.S.S. AL CODA
Coda
(SLOWER)
Fmi7   Abmaj7/Bb   Bb7
life   re-   vealed   in   me.

A Prayer For December

Heavenly Father:
Christmas began
With the gift of your Son
Who in turn gave the world
The gift of His life.
Let me remember, O God,
That Christmas remains
A matter of giving,
Not parties, not presents,
Not material wealth,
For Christmas is Christmas
When I give of myself.

Third Lutheran Church, Louisville, KY

The Gifts Of Christmas

The Gift of Perfect Love

In those days Caesar Augustus issued a decree that a census should be taken of the entire Roman world. (This was the first census that took place while Quirinius was governor of Syria.) And everyone went to his own town to register.

So Joseph also went up from the town of Nazareth in Galilee to Judea, to Bethlehem the town of David, because he belonged to the house and line of David. He went there to register with Mary, who was pledged to be married to him and was expecting a child. While they were there, the time came for the baby to be born, and she gave birth to her firstborn, a son. She wrapped him in cloths and placed him in a manger, because there was no room for them in the inn.

And there were shepherds living out in the fields nearby, keeping watch over their flocks at night. An angel of the Lord appeared to them, and the glory of the Lord shone around them, and they were terrified. But the angel said to them, "Do not be afraid. I bring you good news of great joy that will be for all the people. Today in the town of David a Savior has been born to you; he is Christ the Lord. This will be a sign to you: You will find a baby wrapped in cloths and lying in a manger."

Suddenly a great company of the heavenly host appeared with the angel, praising God and saying,

"Glory to God in the highest,
and on earth peace to men on whom his favor rests."

When the angels had left them and gone into heaven, the shepherds said to one another, "Let's go to Bethlehem and see this thing that has happened, which the Lord has told us about."

So they hurried off and found Mary and Joseph, and the baby, who was lying in the manger. When they had seen him, they spread the word concerning what had been told them about this child, and all who heard it were amazed at what the shepherds said to them. But Mary treasured up all these things and pondered them in her heart. The shepherds returned, glorifying and praising God for all the things they had heard and seen, which were just as they had been told.

Luke 2:1–20

I AM WHO I AM

He has arrived;
  conditions are stable.
Briefly they are visited
  by awestruck strangers
And then, as she holds him
  swaddled tenderly in coarse cloths,
The silent night settles
  as a matter of fact
Around them.

A hammer blow punctuates
  the dense, rabbling air
Of late afternoon. Soon
  the timbre of his last cry
Quakes against
  the night-dark sky.
The grave undertaking is secure,
  until mourners find
His unwrapped linens
  set aside.

Lo, I am with you...

Dwellers near the watering place
  behold him and cherish the sight
As he walks, clothed in light,
  creating out of his love for them
Newness in all things forever.

I am the end...

Be still...I am God.

  Shirley Heeg

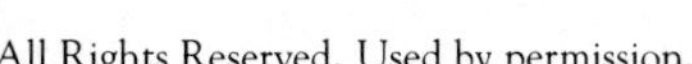

Advent Means Arrival!

*"Arise, shine, for your light has come,
and the glory of the Lord rises upon you.
See, darkness covers the earth
  and thick darkness is over the peoples,
but the Lord rises upon you
  and his glory appears over you.
Nations will come to your light,
  and kings to the brightness of your
  dawn."*

Isaiah 60:1–3

**For Christmas
1985**

*Once again it's Christmas,
and I reach out to you
who waited,
faithful with your love,
until I returned
with semblance of
the one
I used to be
and integrity.*

*It was a bitter turning
that led me far away.
But now,
with this holy season,
I would
come with giving
to place your special treasure
once again with thee.*

Mavis Christensen

SINCE THE EARLY DAYS OF THE CHURCH, God's people have prepared for a proper celebration of Christmas, establishing a season of the church year called Advent. It begins on the fourth Sunday before Christmas and ends on Christmas Eve, the holy night when we celebrate the birth of Christ. This time enables us to prepare our hearts to celebrate the great day our Savior was born.

As a reminder of the power of Christ, Christians have long used Advent wreaths to help them prepare for Christmas. The wreath is covered with Evergreen, a species of tree which is *always* green and the color of life and growth. Our hope for Eternity is *always* sure because it is based on Christ. The wreath is also in the form of a circle which has no beginning and no end. What better way is there to picture Eternity? We need to remember that our life with God is Eternal—now and forever.

As Advent begins we light the first candle, reminding us of God's promises and of a Savior who was to be the Light of the world! The four candles that are found on the edge of the wreath may seem small, but each week the light becomes brighter as we light another candle. On Christmas Eve, the biggest candle—the tall white one in the middle—will be lighted and will tell us that Jesus, the Light in our inky darkness of sin, has been born!

Prayer: Almighty God, throughout all generations, You have given divine direction to all people who would prepare for the coming of Your Son on earth. We ask You now to help us prepare our hearts so that His Spirit can be born in us again. Amen.

Applying the Gift: Our Heavenly Father caused a Light to shine in the darkness of sin.

"Prepare The Way For The Lord"

In the fifteenth year of the reign of Tiberius Caesar–when Pontius Pilate was governor of Judea, Herod tetrarch of Galilee, his brother Philip tetrarch of Iturea and Traconitis, and Lysanias tetrarch of Abilene–during the high priesthood of Annas and Caiaphas, the word of God came to John son of Zechariah in the desert. He went into all the country around the Jordan, preaching a baptism of repentance for the forgiveness of sins. As is written in the book of the words of Isaiah the prophet:

*"A voice of one calling in the desert,
'Prepare the way for the Lord,
  make straight paths for him.
Every valley shall be filled in,
  every mountain and hill made low.
The crooked roads shall become straight,
  the rough ways smooth.
And all mankind will see God's
  salvation.' "*

Luke 3:1–6

JOHN THE BAPTIST tells us to "prepare the way." We are preparing for Christmas in our homes, offices, churches, stores, and schools. Our preparation must include checking our attitudes to make sure they are what God wants them to be. Let us examine ourselves by answering these questions:

• Have we done the very best we can do?

• Have we been kind to those who are less fortunate than ourselves?

• Have we been cheerful in the face of adversity?

• Have we always treated our families with graciousness and respect?

• Have we supported our church with our prayers, our gifts, and our service?

• Have we been appreciative of the beauties of nature that was made possible by our loving heavenly Father?

• Have we been content with the little things of life and not discontented because we wanted more?

• Have we been tolerant of the ideas of others–both the young and the old?

• Have we helped someone along a road that was rougher than our own?

Prayer: Heavenly Father, we ask You to help us to "prepare the way" to make the spiritual journey to Bethlehem in both our hearts and minds. Amen.

Applying the Gift: Have we started our journey to meet Christ?

God's Promise of Christ's Coming: Man's Hope for Salvation

"For to us a child is born,
to us a son is given,
and the government will be on his shoulders.
And he will be called Wonderful Counselor,
Mighty God, Everlasting Father, Prince of Peace."

Isaiah 9:6

GOD'S WORD IS A BOOK OF PROMISE. The promise of the first Advent was given soon after Creation and is found in Genesis 3:15: "And I will put enmity between you and woman, and between your offspring and hers; he will crush your head, and you will strike his heel." This verse promises that in the conflict between good and evil, the Holy Seed Himself will destroy the evil.

We find other promises of the coming of a Messiah in Old Testament prophecies such as, "Therefore the Lord himself will give you a sign: the virgin will be with child and will give birth to a son, and will call him 'Immanuel.'" The name 'Immanuel' means "God with us" and, in interpretation, stands for "God-man." Also, in Micah 5:2 we read, "But you, Bethlehem Ephrathah, though you are small among the clans of Judah, out of you will come for me one who will be ruler over Israel, whose origins are from of old, from ancient times."

Throughout the Jewish history of the Old Testament there are hundreds of prophecies referring to God's promise to send a deliverer. Isaiah 53 is full of the prophetic promises of Christ's coming and subsequent sufferings for the sins of mankind.

Along with the promise of Christ's coming, the scripture also gives the promise of HOPE that man can be delivered from sin, be made right with God, and can enjoy an expectation of eternal salvation. Isaiah 53:6 and 59:16 reveal God's plan for a mediator, His Son, to make this possible.

Christ's coming realized the Hope of salvation and is recorded in the gospel of John 3:16, 17: "For God so loved the world that he gave his one and only Son, that whoever believes in him shall not perish but have eternal life. For God did not send his Son into the world to condemn the world, but to save the world through him."

Prayer: Heavenly Father, thank You for the promise of Your Son. As we commemorate His coming this Advent Season, may our hearts be filled anew with the wonder of Your love for us. Lord Jesus, thank You for coming to earth and giving us Your salvation. Amen.

Applying the Gift: God's promises for man's salvation have come true for each of us. Man's hope for eternal life is real. Do you believe?

When Justice Prevails

A shoot will come up from the stump of
   Jesse;
from his roots a Branch will bear fruit.
The Spirit of the Lord will rest on him—
the Spirit of of wisdom and of
   understanding,
the Spirit of counsel and of power,
the Spirit of knowledge and of the fear of
   the Lord—
and he will delight in the fear of the Lord

He will not judge by what he sees with his
   eyes,
or decide by what he hears with his ears;
but with righteousness he will judge the
   needy,
with justice he will give decisions for the
   poor of the earth.
He will strike the earth with the rod of his
   mouth;
with the breath of his lips he will slay the
   wicked.
Righteousness will be his belt
and faithfulness the sash around his
   waist.

The wolf will live with the lamb,
the leopard will lie down with the goat,
the calf and the lion and the yearling
   together;
and a little child will lead them.
The cow will feed with the bear,
their young will lie down together,
and the lion will eat straw like the ox.
The infant will play near the hole of the
   cobra,
and the young child put his hand into the
   viper's nest.

THIS SCRIPTURE IS PERHAPS BEST KNOWN for its final stanza telling of animals living in peace with each other. The message, however, is closely connected to the earlier verses and also with Isaiah 9:6–7.

The first five verses tell us about a king who is coming and on whom rests the Spirit of God. This king will be concerned with justice and equity, pointing to Christ, who perfectly fulfills this passage. The Scripture tells us that He will not judge according to the standards of the world but that He will judge the poor and the meek with justice; that he will be a king who hears God and is obedient to His will; that He is God of the poor and weak and those in need of help; and that He is to be a king who does not cater to the rich and powerful, but to the needy and powerless.

In the next four verses, we have that marvelous picture of animals of all kinds peacefully co-existing. The pairs consist of one weak animal and one powerful one—for example, a wolf (adult) and a lamb (baby). The weak and helpless humans—the toddlers and infants—are here pictured as playing in safety among the deadly snakes; again we have a picture of concern for the weak. God's concern, as seen in the king and in this picture of paradise is for the weak, helpless, and meek of the earth. He is their protector.

Although Christ has perfectly fulfilled this passage in Himself, His kingdom, one of justice for all and special concern for the weak and helpless, has not fully come. We are now living in the time when this passage has already been fulfilled in Christ but it has not yet been fulfilled in our world. Our hope is for the fulfillment of this passage in this world.

Prayer: God, help us to live in concern for justice for the poor and weak. We use the king in this Book of Promises as our example to live in obedience to You and with concern that justice and righteousness will be done. Amen.

Applying the Gift: The Lion of God protects the lamb.

They will neither harm nor destroy on all
   my holy mountain,
for the earth will be full of the knowledge
   of the Lord
as the waters cover the sea.
          Isaiah 11:1–9

For Unto Us A Child Is Born

Ab Eb   Ab Csus4 C   F   G/F   Gmi/F   F
Of the
Fmaj7   Gmi/F   3   Fadd9   Bb/c
in-crease of his gov-ern-ment and peace there shall be no end   On
Fmaj7   Gmi/F   Fadd9
Da-vid's throne with justice and judg-ment hence-forth for-ev — er — and
Bb/c   Ab   Eb   Ab Eb   Ab   Eb
ev - er.   For un-to us a child is   born,   and un-to us a son is-
Ab   Eb Ab   Eb   Ab Eb Ab   Eb
— giv — en. —   For un-to us a child is   born,   and un-to us a son is
Ab   Eb Ab   Eb   Ab   Eb
— giv — en. —   The might-y God — ev-er last-ing Fa-ther;
Ab   Eb Ab   C   3   Fadd9 G/F Gmi/F   Fadd9
the Prince of Peace   Prince of Peace   and the peo-ple shall
F   G/F   Gmi/F Fadd9   F   G/F
know and the peo-ple shall know. —   And the peo-ple shall know. — And the peo-ple shall
Gmi/F   F
know. —

Fair?

FAIR—WHAT IS FAIR and who is fair?

Is God fair? Sometimes our faith falters and we ask this question. Maybe we should ask instead, is He merciful?

He says He will never make our yoke too heavy to bear.

When my children were young and before I came to know Jesus, it was easy for me to say, "Now we have to be fair; there are three of you, so you have to share," or, "One gets new shoes today and the others have to wait their turn."

Christmas was easy, too, for we had only so much money to spend and at that time the only meaning of Christmas was presents under the tree. So everything in our lives revolved around the mighty dollar.

Now that I have come to know Jesus and His gift, I know it is not something I can give to my children or anyone. The most precious gift of all is not mine to give and cannot be bought even by the wealthy. It is freely offered and given for the asking. I invited Jesus into my life and a whole new world opened for me—it is like smelling the roses for the first time—appreciating all the little things as well as the big and knowing it is all from the Lord. He is always there for us, waiting to be asked into our lives.

Now I would like to open that new world to my family. I wish that I could lay it down by the Christmas tree, and Christmas morning they would open their eyes and see what I see. God works in His own time schedule and yes, He is merciful. I know with prayer and through faith, and by giving Him all the glory, my family will open their eyes and accept His gift as I did.

Maybe they have to suffer a little first. Maybe the times I felt were not fair were the times I needed to open my eyes. My children and grandchildren are going through their growing period now, and perhaps through my learning and loving and God's merciful and generous love and understanding they will see His light sooner than I did.

Prayer: Lord, give us strength and wisdom to spread Your word and open the eyes of the world to Your gift. Amen.

Applying the Gift: The Lord God mercifully gave His only begotten Son, Jesus, for our salvation, as a gift, just for the asking. Show us who to tell about this precious gift.

Building On A (Traditional?) Foundation

I have been reminded of your sincere faith, which first lived in your grandmother Lois and in your mother Eunice and, I am persuaded, now lives in you also. For this reason I remind you to fan into flame the gift of God, which is in you through the laying on of my hands. For God did not give us a spirit of timidity, but a spirit of power, of love and of self-discipline.

II Timothy 1: 5–7

Nevertheless, God's solid foundation stands firm, sealed with this inscription: "The Lord knows those who are his," and, "Everyone who confesses the name of the Lord must turn away from wickedness."

II Timothy 2:19

SINCE MY FATHER is a carpenter, I have a real appreciation of the importance of a good foundation. Not only must a foundation be firm, it must be true (level and square).

In building our family traditions at Christmas time, we must always seek to place them squarely upon the foundation laid by God through his Son, Jesus. Therefore, any activity we do must build upon the importance of Christ in our lives. Here are a few of the themes and activities upon which we are striving to build.

On the first Sunday in Advent, our church family makes advent wreathes. The wreath is rich in symbolism—eternal (circle and evergreens), light of the world (candles), love, joy, hope, and peace (4 candles), preparation and expectation (the four candles are purple), and the centrality of Christ (white Christ candle), just to name a few. Our church participants bring a bag of greens from home so each wreath takes on a special sense of "family." This wreath then becomes a constant presence and reminder in our homes through the season.

God expects us to give others kindness and goodness. Keeping our resources to ourselves is opposed to the spirit of Christmas. We want our family to be mindful of others. We strive to give more of ourselves and our abilities; this means taking time for others. Our preschool boys enjoy caroling, and their presence brings a smile to young and old alike. Also, a grace gift can help us to be more grateful for what we have, as opposed to what we give away. We make a special monetary gift to those in need. In addition, we try to give homemade gifts that express our relationship and love to the receivers. We must be courageous in leading our families and churches to build upon the foundation of Jesus by sowing seeds of caring, selflessness, sharing, and peace. The first gift of Christmas was God giving Himself to others. Let us strive to do likewise.

Prayer: Dear Heavenly Father, as we prepare for Christmas, help us to remember that You gave Yourself to us as the first gift. Guide us to build our Christmas celebrations in ways that will show love for You and those around us. In Jesus' Name. Amen.

Applying the Gift: The only way to receive the blessing of the season is to give yourself away.

Christmas Decorations

I READ IN TODAY'S PAPER that they are putting Christmas decorations up in Hollywood. That seems quite strange to me, since today is October 7! Our celebration of Christmas has become very commercial. Even we as Christians sometimes are so caught up in buying gifts, untangling garland, and putting lights around the house that we forget what we are celebrating. We start early, but still find ourselves hustling around on December 23, and forgetting to prepare the most important thing, our hearts!

Advent is the time of preparation. The word Advent comes from two Latin words meaning come and to. It is the time of year when Christians begin to think of when Jesus "came to" earth. It is the time for us to prepare our hearts for Him.

I would like to suggest that we focus on four significant words that can help us prepare our hearts for Him: forgiveness, peace, joy, and love.

When we think of the main reason Jesus came to earth, we think of forgiveness. He came to bring God's forgiveness, and He taught us to forgive one another as God has forgiven us. Is there someone you need to forgive this Advent season to prepare your heart for Jesus?

Jesus brought peace to us—a peace far greater than we can imagine. It is a peace we can have when we live as Jesus taught us to live. Do you need to find that inner peace in your life?

Next focus on the joy that Jesus brought to Mary and Joseph, to the Hebrews that knew Him, and down through the generations to all of us who know Him as our Savior. We can prepare our hearts by sensing this joy and sharing it with others.

Finally, let us meditate on love. God in his great and infinite love, sent His Son, Jesus, that we could have life more abundantly and that we could understand how God wants us to love one another. Are you loving others this Christmas season the way Christ has taught us to love?

Begin now to prepare your heart for Christ's coming, and to celebrate the forgiveness, peace, joy, and love that He brought to us.

Prayer: Dear Lord, help us to prepare our hearts and decorate our lives for the celebration of Your birth. We thank You for Your gifts of forgiveness, peace, joy, and love that You have brought us. Thank You, too, for coming into our lives and living within us so that we can share these gifts with others. Amen.

Applying the Gift: List specific examples of how you are giving or receiving these gifts in your life.

Great Anticipation

THE GREAT HOPE OF ALL CHRISTIANS is that one day we will be in Heaven. We do not know exactly what Heaven will be like, but we do know this; 1) we will see God, 2) we will know the things we did not know before, and 3) we will have a right relationship with Him.

God rightfully belongs first in all our lives. Part of the beauty of the Christian life here on earth is that we now and then see "glimpses of Heaven," through fellowship and love, the beauty of nature, good music, or perhaps a moment of pure honesty with God. If we are honest with ourselves, we see that there are often things that prevent us from the pure joy of a "glimpse of Heaven." These "things" may be anything that we place higher on our list of loves than God. God has created many pleasures for us here in this life; however, and here is the main point, they were never meant to take the place of the One who created them. Nothing, not self, family, friends, career, hobbies, sports, can ever be more important than the Creator.

A contemporary Christian singer, Phil Keaggy, has summed up well the type of life that leads to the great anticipation of Heaven:

"Holding conversation with a friend I know is there,
  Great anticipation fills my soul.
  It fills my heart,
  It fills the air
  all the day.
  And the wind is at my back.

Nothing in this world can take Your place,
  All the pride of man laid low,
  And all his works of gold,
  Nothing can compare with what You are.
  Let everything else go,
  Let it go."*

Prayer: God, help me to put my priorities in order. I will begin by putting You first. Help me to order the other areas of my life properly. In Jesus' name. Amen.

Applying the Gift: When God is first in our lives, we live in great anticipation of the day we will see Him face to face.

Now we see but a poor reflection as in a mirror; then we shall see face to face. Now I know in part; then I shall know fully, even as I am fully known.

I Corinthians 13:12

Not a lofty
evergreen
bejeweled with lights
costly gifts
beneath;
but a tree
stripped of its branches
made into a cross
stark, ugly
makes known God's love.
Gifts beneath:
joy, peace, forgiveness
Life eternal.
Come...Receive...*

Leota Campbell

*Used by permission from *Living Values,* published by Good News Publishers, Westchester, IL 60153

She opens her arms to the poor
  and extends her hands to the needy.
When it snows, she has no fear for her
  household;
  for all of them are clothed in scarlet.
She makes coverings for her bed;
  she is clothed in fine linen and purple.
Her husband is respected at the city gate,
  where he takes his seat among the
  elders of the land.
She makes linen garments and sells them,
  and supplies the merchants with
  sashes.
She is clothed with strength and dignity;
  she can laugh at the days to come.
She speaks with wisdom,
  and faithful instruction is on her
  tongue.
She watches over the affairs of her
  household
  and does not eat the bread of idleness.
Her children arise and call her blessed;
  her husband also, and he praises her:
"Many women do noble things,
  but you surpass them all."
Charm is deceptive, and beauty is
  fleeting;
  but a woman who fears the Lord is to
  be praised.
  Proverbs 31: 20–31

To Grandmother's House For Christmas

FOR MONTHS WE CALIFORNIANS planned our Christmas trip to Minnesota. Boots and mufflers were borrowed, mittens and coats purchased and red velvet dresses sewn. A little friend loaned a pink checked snowsuit for baby sister.

What a disappointment to the five Californians to find no snow on the ground as we looked down on Minneapolis from the airplane windows. But we were not disappointed for long. We awoke the next morning at a friend's home to gently falling snow. Soon a white mantle covered the ground—and it snowed, and snowed, and yes, snowed some more.

The days filled with activity left us with memories of Grandpa on the old sled with red runners racing down the crowded hill west of Mapleton, and the baby enveloped in the pink checked snowsuit and wrapped in blankets while bumping along on the sled pulled by Grandpa or big sisters; for by now, the snow piles had grown mountainous and walking uptown for the daily mail and groceries was much easier than driving. Shoveling snow became the family exercise, something new for California-raised girls.

Grandma's kitchen was the gathering place for reading Christmas cards, hearing the latest uptown news—such as "whose snow-mobile was making all that noise last evening," and devouring her wonderful, rich delicacies. Her pantry contained hidden treasures such as frosted chocolate cookies in a round tin behind the jack-pine doors of the high cupboards. Everyone knew they were there, nestled between layers of wax paper, but I think she secretly loved our "finding" them and our exclamations of appreciation. Her son's carved wood highchair had been brought down from the attic for baby. It looked right in place in that cozy old-fashioned kitchen; now, the family was complete again. The green wreath covered with snow and capped with a red bow hanging on her front door that Christmas gave notice to those who entered that all was well inside. Three generations gathered round the table, preparing to gather before the Christmas tree for the anticipated gift exchange.

Not many years later Grandma was gone too soon, missed by friends and family. Her chocolate cookies, the kitchen which had conveyed delectable promises of satisfaction, and her warm hospitality and chuckle of that special Christmas were now in the past. However, they live on in our memories and in the traits carried over into the lives of her son and granddaughters.

That son was the only survivor of the larger family she yearned for—but three children were to be his to fulfill her dreams. Her laughter and life were stilled, but God had heard her prayers and surrounded her with a complete circle of love and hope for future generations.

Prayer: Dear God, we praise You for giving us family love and memories, joy and laughter. We praise You for being with us in times of sorrow. Help us to remember to pray for our families and love them as You do. Amen.

Applying the Gift: Search for a hidden goody of love to give each of your loved ones this Christmas.

Lord, you have been our dwelling place
throughout all generations.
Before the mountains were born
or you brought forth the earth and the
world,
from everlasting to everlasting you are
God.

You turn men back to dust, saying,
"Return to dust, O sons of men."
Psalm 90: 1, 2

"Charlie Brown" Christmas Trees

Your beauty should not come from out-ward adornment, such as braided hair and the wearing of gold jewelry and fine clothes. Instead, it should be that of your inner self, the unfading beauty of a gentle and quiet spirit, which is of great worth in God's sight.

I Peter 3: 3, 4

But if anyone obeys his word, God's love is truly made complete in him. This is how we know we are in him: Whoever claims to live in him must walk as Jesus did.

I John 2: 5

Keep on loving each other as brothers.

Hebrews 13: 1

It was actually about three years, but it seemed like forever. That is how long we lived in our small mobile home. In fact, it was so dinky that I shared a room with my five year old brother. The first Christmas there, my family got a "Charlie Brown" Christmas tree because it was the only tree that could fit our tiny living room.

Do you remember that Charlie Brown Christmas Special which plays on television each year? Well, a segment shows Charlie Brown buying a small, dilapidated Christmas tree even though he could have bought a big aluminum tree. His delicate pine could not even hold a glittery Christmas decoration. At the end, however, the Peanuts gang bands together and gives the little tree love and cherishing warmth, and it grows tall and strong, holding many lights, bulbs, and stars.

At first, I was somewhat embarrassed at our ramshackle tree, but then I thought of the Spirit of Christmas. It should not matter what people think about your tree and the worldly Christmas things, but it should matter what Jesus thinks of you and the spiritual Christmas things.

As I kept thinking, I realized that, in a way, we are all "Charlie Brown" Christmas trees. God gives us love and warmth, and with God's Son, Jesus, we flourish and are made strong through Him. Ironically, we, the trees, are supposed to decorate ourselves, but not with glittery balls, fancy snow, or flashing lights. God wants us to bear the fruits of the Spirit which are "…love, joy, peace, patience, kindness, goodness, faithfulness, gentleness, and self control. Against such things there is no law." (Galatians, 5: 22, 23) Jesus makes our "branches and needles" shine with our inner beauty. This keeps us from caring what other people think of us.

After Jesus makes us flourish, we should help other "Charlie Brown" trees flourish with God's love. We do this by talking about Jesus and helping them in any way we can. He has made us competent ministers of a New Covenant (Jesus Christ): not of the Letter (Mosaic Law), but of the Spirit, for the letter kills but the Spirit gives Life.

Now my family lives in a big house and is able to buy a huge tree during Christmas. Come to think of it, Baby Jesus did not have a Christmas tree, and if He did He would probably pick out a humble but dignified evergreen like Charlie Brown!

Prayer: Dear Jesus, make our lives "shine" with Your fruits, so we can help the "Charlie Brown" trees around us grow tall and strong. Amen.

Applying the Gift: What decorations do you have to share?

In The Pits

A voice of one calling:
"In the desert prepare the way for the
  Lord;
make straight in the wilderness a highway
  for our God.
Every valley shall be raised up,
  every mountain and hill made low;
the rough ground shall become level,
  the rugged places a plain.
And the glory of the Lord will be
  revealed,
  and all mankind together will see it.

For the mouth of the Lord has spoken."

A voice says, "Cry out."
  And I said, "What shall I cry?"
"All men are like grass,
  and all their glory is like the flowers of
  the field.
The grass withers and the flowers fall,
  because the breath of the Lord blows
  on them.
The grass withers and the flowers fall,
  But the word of our God stands
  forever."

You who bring good tidings to Zion,
  go up on a high mountain.
You who bring good tidings to Jerusalem,
  lift up your voice with a shout,
lift it up, do not be afraid;
  say to the towns of Judah, "Here is
your God!"

Every so often, it seems, each one of us experiences an emotional or spiritual low in life, a time "in the pits." Maybe things have not "gone my way," someone has hurt my feelings, or through thoughtlessness or anger, I have hurt someone else. "Pits" is a term that we often use for these low times, and we prefer not to remember them. When we think of the opposites–"peak" or "mountain-top" experiences, we can usually recall some very positive times.

Not only do individuals have peaks and valleys. Nations, cities, and societies have them, too. Sometimes as we travel through a community or city we find that it is in a valley, economically, even though physical maps would show no valley at all. There are moral valleys, as well, and there are traps for people and societies.

When a person is "in the pits" emotionally, spiritually, or even morally, the encouragement and support of friends and family can be very helpful on the climb back toward the peak. The same holds true for a society. What about your area? Is it in a moral valley?

As we prepare the way for the Lord this Advent season, let us encourage and support those movements in our areas, families and friends that will help lift us from "the pits."

Prayer: Give us strength, Lord, to be encouragers of all people and societies that we touch, that we may be ready to receive You. Amen.

Applying Our Gift: Who needs a "lift" from you today?

See, the Sovereign Lord comes with
  power,
  and his arm rules for him.
See, his reward is with him,
  and his recompense accompanies him.
He tends his flock like a shepherd:
  He gathers the lambs in his arms
and carries them close to his heart;
he gently leads those that have young.
                    Isaiah 40: 3–11

Standing On The Promises

And now the Lord says—he who formed
* me in the womb to be his servant*
to bring Jacob back to him and gather
* Israel to himself,*
for I am honored in the eyes of the Lord
* and my God has been my strength—*
he says: "It is too small a thing for you to
* be my servant*
*   to restore the tribes of Jacob*
*   and bring back those of Israel I have*
* kept.*
I will also make you a light for the
* Gentiles.*
*   that you may bring my salvation to the*
* ends of the earth."*
This is what the Lord says—the Redeemer
* and Holy One of Israel—*
*   to him who was despised and abhorred*
* by the nation,*
*   to the servant of rulers:*
* "Kings will see you and rise up,*
* princes will see and bow down,*
* because of the Lord, who is faithful,*
* the Holy One of Israel, who has cho-*
* sen you."*

Isaiah 49:5–7

SEVEN CENTURIES BEFORE THE LORD JESUS was born in Bethlehem, Isaiah wrote the words we find in today's Scripture reading. Consider the four areas of promises found in the verses.

His coming birth was announced. Luke 1 records the angel's visit to Mary, telling that her Son, whose name was to be Jesus, would be the Son of God. The great prophet Isaiah told of this announcement too, and of the promise of a coming Redeemer. Also, God defined His mission. Jesus would regather Israel and rule over Jacob. He would be the light for salvation to the Gentiles and all peoples of the earth. Isaiah tells us that Jesus would be misunderstood and would suffer rejection, even death, but that finally He would be recognized and worshipped by all nations and peoples.

These promises have been fulfilled—at least in part—showing us God's faithfulness. Would a God of such order and detail be less faithful to us? Let's look at promises for us in the New Testament paralleling each of those we read in Isaiah.

First, when we accept in faith as Mary did, we are promised new life, to be new creations in Christ (II Corinthians 5:17). Second, Jesus promised the Holy Spirit to guide us so we can do even greater works than He did (John 14:12). Third, in His prayer to our Father, Jesus said that we would be hated by the world, and He prayed for our protection (John 17). Finally, He promised victory now and told us that we will rule with Him when He comes again (I Corinthians 6:2).

God's promises without our faith are only words on a page. Standing on the testimony of the Old Testament, Mary accepted, with faith, God's promises. Her Son was born, as God promised, and He's our Christ, our Savior and Lord. We have much more testimony than Mary for our stand of faith!

> "Standing on the promises, I cannot fall,
>   List'ning every moment to the Savior's call,
>   Resting in my Savior as my all in all,
>   Standing on the promises of God."*

Prayer: Father God, we see Your faithfulness to keep the promises You have made. We trust You to do this in our lives, too. In Jesus' Name. Amen.

Applying the Gift: Faith makes God's promises alive and real!

*Hymn—"Standing on the Promises"
  Text: R. Kelso Carter

Trust in the Lord with all your heart and lean not on your own understanding;
in all your ways acknowledge him, and he will make your paths straight.

Proverbs 3: 5, 6

The Recipe For Serenity

ADVENT...

The season for remembrances...traditions...the joy of my heritage...South Dakota prairies...golden fields of waving wheat, so beautiful in the sun...Bethlehem Lutheran Church...the Sunday School pump organ...Norwegian cookies, Nels Larson and Lars Nelson(!)...Norwegian flat bread...Norwegian fish...things past.

I was born in Aberdeen, then a small city. The corner store was at the end of the alley from us, and I was often sent there for a loaf of "Holsum" bread. We went to Sunday School every Sunday (my mother was the Superintendent). At Christmas, or at least around that time, our church gave its big Lutefisk dinner for around sixteen hundred people. I still have a recipe book from the church that gives amounts needed to serve that many people! After long prayers of thanksgiving for the wonderful Norwegian food, we stuffed ourselves with fish in cream sauce drizzled with butter, boiled potatoes, peas and carrots, and wonderful cookies with rice pudding topped with raspberry sauce. What a feast! These same traditions for cooking Norwegian foods were carried on by my dear Irish mother all the years of my life. Today I, too, am sharing these traditions with my children. How precious they are, these things long gone from our busy society. How happy I am each year to return to these familiar traditions. One summer my daughter asked me why I did not make those Norwegian tortillas in the summer time. She was talking about the flat bread called "lefse," which is indeed shaped like a tortilla, made very much the same but of a dough of mashed potato.

Norwegian and Irish families abound in the Dakotas. Both nationalities settled there as farmers years ago. The intermarrying was inevitable. Since it was Depression time when I was growing up, finances were slim. Did I know that? No. I was rich in family. I had no idea that there was any better food than what we had. The winters were long and cold, and the wind across the prairie had us dressed with only eyes exposed to see our way to school. We spent our days on our sleds, no matter the weather. Good times!

I remember the eleven o'clock Christmas Eve service, (so beautiful to see through the tired eyes of a child of ten), the Sunday school play, and church picnics on the farm of a parishioner. That lovely faith nurtured in those days of cherished traditions has not been forgotten. The learning process begun and primed over and over keeps me in good stead. A need is filled day after day. I praise God for the days gone by and for great family heritages.

Prayer:

God my Father, hear my prayer,
Guide me through the day so fair.
Let my lips no evil speak,
Let my heart be pure and meek.
Guide my feet in paths of light,
Let my hands work for the right.
Fill my soul with love of Thee;
All day, Lord, walk Thou with me.

Applying the Gift: Let us praise God for our family heritages, a reminder of our inheritance in Christ Jesus.

Let Us Talk About Jesus

Now there were some Greeks among those who went up to worship at the Feast. They came to Philip, who was from Bethsaida in Galilee, with a request. "Sir," they said, "we would like to see Jesus." Philip went to tell Andrew; Andrew and Philip in turn told Jesus.

Jesus replied, "The hour has come for the Son of Man to be glorified. I tell you the truth, unless a kernel of wheat falls to the ground and dies, it remains only a single seed. But if it dies, it produces many seeds. The man who loves his life will lose it, while the man who hates his life in this world will keep it for eternal life. Whoever serves me must follow me; and where I am, my servant also will be. My Father will honor the one who serves me."

John 12: 20–26

A little girl was riding in a car with her father. She turned to her father and asked him, "Daddy, is it all right to talk about Jesus?"

Her father was a little surprised by her question, but he answered, "Why, yes, it's all right to talk about Jesus."

There was silence for a while. Then the little girl said with assurance and finality in her voice, "Well, then, let's talk about Jesus."

As Christians we talk about many things during a day—the weather, politics, sports, and, sometimes, the cost of food. During this Advent season, let us talk about Jesus!

About His redeeming love:

His gift of salvation and peace;

His life, His teachings, His goodness;

His compassion for everybody.

It is so easy to talk about many lesser matters, but during this season, let us think and talk about our Lord, who was born to bring life, love, and peace to everyone, everywhere.

Prayer: Gracious God, thank You for Your wonderful love, the great hope You have given, and for the new life You gave us through Your gift of Jesus. Amen.

Applying the Gift: Through the gift of Jesus Christ, God makes us all into one family.

Follow The Star

"But you, Bethlehem Ephrathah,
though you are small among the clans
of Judah,
out of you will come for me
one who will be ruler over Israel,
whose origins are from old,
from ancient times."

Micah 5: 2

After Jesus was born in Bethlehem in Judea...

Matthew 2: 1a

So Naomi returned from Moab, accompanied by Ruth the Moabitess, her daughter-in-law, arriving in Bethlehem as the barley harvest was beginning.

Ruth 1: 22

Hᴀᴠᴇ ʏᴏᴜ ʙᴇᴇɴ ᴛᴏ Bᴇᴛʜʟᴇʜᴇᴍ? God calls us to that ancient and historic city. Many people have gone before us; it is a well-traveled road. Naomi and Ruth arrived there, without family and in poverty. They found a harvest in Boaz's field, and Ruth became his wife, the mother of his son, and entered into the blood line of Christ. Her great-grandson David was annointed for kingship (I Samuel 16) in that little town. Joseph and Mary found only a lowly place to rest and became loving parents of a promised babe, the ruler over Israel (Luke 2). The shepherds (Luke 2:15) and Magi (Matthew 2:1) found the holy child of Bethlehem under a bright star. These travelers responded in obedience, love and worship to the promises of the little town of Bethlehem.

Prayer: O holy child of Bethlehem,
Descend on us, we pray;
Cast out our sin and enter in,
Be born in us today.
We hear the Christmas angels
The great glad tidings tell,
O come to us, abide with us,
Our Lord Emmanuel. *   Amen.

Applying the Gift: We rejoice as Christ abides with us on our journey to Bethlehem allowing us to share in the harvest, to receive and give love, to worship the glory of Israel: God's Son Jesus born in Bethlehem in Judea.

*Christmas carol "O Little Town of Bethlehem."
Words by Phillip Brooks.

At that time Mary got ready and hurried to a town in the hill country of Judea, where she entered Zechariah's home and greeted Elizabeth. When Elizabeth heard Mary's greeting, the baby leaped in her womb, and Elizabeth was filled with the Holy Spirit. In a loud voice she exclaimed: "Blessed are you among women, and blessed is the child you will bear! But why am I so favored that the mother of my Lord should come to me? As soon as the sound of your greeting reached my ears, the baby in my womb leaped for joy. Blessed is she who has believed that what the Lord has said to her will be accomplished!"

And Mary said:
"My soul glorifies the Lord
  and my spirit rejoices in God my Savior,
for he has been mindful
  of the humble state of his servant.
From now on all generations will call me blessed,
  for the Mighty One has done great things for me—
  holy is his name.

His mercy extends to those who fear him,
  from generation to generation.
He has performed mighty deeds with his arm;
  he has scattered those who are proud in their inmost thoughts,
He has brought down rulers from their thrones
  but has lifted up the humble.
He has filled the hungry with good things
  but has sent the rich away empty.
He has helped his servant Israel,
  remembering to be merciful
to Abraham and his descendants forever,
  even as he said to our fathers."

Mary stayed with Elizabeth for about three months and then returned home.

Luke 1: 39–56

God Cares For All

IN THIS PASSAGE WE FIND two women singing the praises of God. First Elizabeth speaks, blessing Mary for what God is doing through her. She calls Mary "the mother of my Lord," thereby recognizing the special place Jesus has for us all. Mary responds with the poem called the "Magnificat." In this song she declares the greatness of God. She sees God's greatness in the things He has done.

We see God's concern for the humble in the way He chose to be born into this world. As the ruler of the universe, He could have chosen to be born into the family of the rulers of the time. Instead He chose the family of a carpenter. Mary speaks of her humble position in life, her low estate. She was not the daughter of a wealthy or important family. Yet God looked with favor on her and chose her to be the mother of His Son. God is concerned for those who are disadvantaged, who are scorned by others. He has concern for the widow, the orphan, and the poor. God is a god of the humble, not the haughty.

While the Magnificat is written in the past tense, it points to what God is doing now and what He will do in the future. God's care and concern for the disadvantaged continues in all times and places. In His ministry, Jesus walked among the poor and helped those in need.

Mary is an example of a great biblical theme: she not only looks back on the great things God has done for those who are of humble position, she also looks forward to the continuous work of God and His constant care for those who are widows, orphans, poor, aliens, and disadvantaged.

Prayer: God, thank You that You care for the humble, the needy, and the hurting. Thank You for being a God of the humble and for coming to earth as a humble man. Continue to be with all of us in our needs. Amen.

Applying the Gift: God cares for even the lowliest of people.

Suffering Children

People were bringing little children to Jesus to have him touch them, but the disciples rebuked them. When Jesus saw this, he was indignant. He said to them, "Let the little children come to me, and do not hinder them, for the kingdom of God belongs to such as these. I tell you the truth, anyone who will not receive the kingdom of God like a little child will never enter it." And he took the children in his arms, put his hands on them and blessed them.

Mark 10: 13–16

CHRISTMAS HAS BEEN MADE into a holiday for children. Stores and toy manufacturers continue to appeal to the insatiable desire of a child for more new toys that do more new things. All this tinsel and glitter seem to call from every corner for children to come join in. I think the story of the first Christmas lends itself to this cultural deluge—the sweet innocent Christ-child lying in a manger of hay, gently cooing as the wise men present their gifts to Him.

Let us, as Christians, remember that this is not just a child's holiday. This is truly a holy day for everyone. This is not a day which only invites the children to be joyous, this is a day which invites everyone to experience a deep peace and joy. Do not let the commercial appeal to children cause you to miss the grown-up embrace of God's love.

Prayer: Dear Heavenly Father, help us, we pray, to come with the awe of the shepherds and the humility of the wise men to the cradle of the King. Through Jesus we pray. Amen.

Applying the Gift: We can only see the joy of Christmas when we look through the eyes of a child at the one Holy Child.

Come, Share the Lord

W*HEN WE ACCEPT* J*ESUS*, we also accept an invitation to a wedding feast at the marriage of the Church and the Lamb of God, and our hope of heaven becomes a reality.

Christmas and other family celebrations such as weddings are times of joy and anticipation. We ready our homes, prepare special food and clothes, and budget our time. We buy gifts for special people and rejoice in the season and the reason. And as the Scripture says, the bride of Christ—the Church—must also be made ready.

Sometimes it seems as if family celebrations are disasters. Once we were burglarized during a family wedding. That could have spoiled the day, but our daughter was still married, evidenced by the fact that the first time she signed her new name was on a police report. No one met the thief face to face or lost anything irreplaceable, for which we are thankful.

At times it seems as if my Christian walk is also a disaster. How can I possibly be considered one of the saints of the Church performing righteous acts and hoping to wear fine, bright and clean linen, to share in the eternal wedding feast? The Apostle Paul gives the answer: "But now he has reconciled you by Christ's physical body through death to present you holy in his sight, without blemish and free from accusation—if you continue in your faith, established and firm not moved from the hope held out in the gospel." (Colossians 1: 22, 23)

We long for family celebrations to be joyous, free of disasters, and perfect in every way. We also long to be present at the eternal feast, sharing in the oneness symbolized on earth in holy matrimony. When Christ is present, that is possible no matter what happens.

Prayer: Dear Jesus, we ask You to be present in our hearts and homes during this holiday season. Lord, make us one in love as we meet together to celebrate your birthday and the promised feast in heaven. Amen.

Applying the Gift: Look for and ask a lonely person to share in Your family celebration during the holidays, and continue to remember them during the whole year.

"Hallelujah!
*   For the Lord God Almighty reigns.*
Let us rejoice and be glad
*   and give him glory!*
For the wedding of the Lamb has come,
*   and his bride has made herself ready.*
Fine linen, bright and clean,
*   was given her to wear."*

"Blessed are those who are invited to the
wedding supper of the Lamb!"
*   Revelation 19:6b–8, 9*

In Christ there is no East or West,   *Join hands the, brothers of the faith,*
In Him no South or North,   *Whate'er your race may be;*
But one great fellowship of love   *Who serves my Father as a son*
Throughout the whole wide earth.   *Is surely kin to me.**

**Words by John Oxenham, 1852–1941, by permission of Desmond Dunkerley.*

What Wondrous Love Is This

2. When I was sinking down, sinking down, sinking down,
When I was sinking down, sinking down,
When I was sinking down beneath God's righteous frown,
Christ laid aside His crown for my soul, for my soul,
Christ laid aside His crown for my soul.

3. To God and to the Lamb I will sing, I will sing,
To God and to the Lamb I will sing,
To God and to the Lamb Who is the great "I Am,"
While millions join the theme, I will sing, I will sing,
While millions join the theme, I will sing.

4. And when from death I'm free, I'll sing on, I'll sing on,
And when from death I'm free, I'll sing on,
And when from death I'm free, I'll sing and joyful be,
And thro' eternity I'll sing on, I'll sing on,
And thro' eternity I'll sing on.

Joy To The World

The Word became flesh and made his dwelling among us. We have seen his glory, the glory of the One and Only, who came from the Father, full of grace and truth.

John 1:14

Rejoice in the Lord always. I will say it again: Rejoice! Let your gentleness be evident to all. The Lord is near. Do not be anxious about anything, but in everything, by prayer and petition, with thanksgiving, present your requests to God. And the peace of God, which transcends all understanding, will guard your hearts and your minds in Christ Jesus.

Finally, brothers, whatever is true, whatever is noble, whatever is right, whatever is pure, whatever is lovely, whatever is admirable–if anything is excellent or praiseworthy–think about such things. Whatever you have learned or received or heard from me, or seen in me–put it into practice. And the God of peace will be with you.

Philippians 4: 4–9

As we prepare for Christmas, we can joyfully accept the presence of God in Christ Jesus and then in us. "God among us" is always a reason for rejoicing. We need to feel this joy in times of difficulty as well as in times of celebration.

Paul tells us to fill our minds with good things; this is not as easy as filling our Christmas tins with goodies. Examine your thinking; make sure your thoughts are true, honorable, just, gracious, and of things worthy of praise.

The Bible says "The Word of God became a human being and lived among us." The very thought that God loved us so much that He came to us and knows all about our human problems should make us very joyful.

God sent Jesus to be His representative, and He sent Him as all of us began life–as a little baby. Later, Jesus mingled in the markets, visited in the prisons, and left this world fully aware of all the problems that humans face. Because He shared this human life, we can know that He understands mankind. We know, too, that because He lived here on Earth and died for us, we can call Him Master instead of Mister.

Our hearts should be humble and full of Joy when we realize that God lived with us–and still does!

Prayer: Loving God, help us to celebrate Christmas by being aware that You are with us right now. May Your presence in our lives make a visible difference in our relationships and help us to reflect the transforming love You gave us through Your Son. Amen.

Applying the Gift: Look around; God lives with us!

The Heaven-Sent Scent

So I say, live by the Spirit, and you will not gratify the desires of the sinful nature. For the sinful nature desires what is contrary to the Spirit, and the Spirit what is contrary to the sinful nature. They are in conflict with each other, so that you do not do what you want. But if you are led by the Spirit, you are not under law.

The acts of the sinful nature are obvious: sexual immorality, impurity and debauchery; idolatry and witchcraft; hatred, discord, jealousy, fits of rage, selfish ambition, dissensions, factions and envy; drunkenness, orgies, and the like. I warn you, as I did before, that those who live like this will not inherit the kingdom of God.

But the fruit of the Spirit is love, joy, peace, patience, kindness, goodness, faithfulness, gentleness and self-control. Against such things there is no law. Those who belong to Christ Jesus have crucified the sinful nature with its passions and desires. Since we live by the Spirit, let us keep in step with the Spirit. Let us not become conceited, provoking and envying each other.

Galatians 5: 16–26

I RECENTLY PULLED A WINTER SWEATER out of its summer hibernation in a cedar lined drawer. The rich fresh fragrance of cedar pervaded the entire garment. The long extended exposure to the cedar had allowed the scent to permeate the threads.

During the Advent season, we have an opportunity for an extended exposure to the Christ-child. Too often, the glitter and commercialism wear us down and rather than absorbing the true spirit of the season, we insulate ourselves from the noise of the season. (Callousness, cynicism and sin eat holes in our lives like a moth in a wool mill.)

Advent gives us the same opportunity the sweater had, to enjoy an extended and an intense exposure to a much needed preservative. We need to spend more time with God during this holiday than we do shopping, wrapping, and partying. In His presence, His Spirit permeates our lives and produces love, joy, peace, patience, gentleness, faithfulness and self-control.

Prayer: Dear God, we pray that during this holiday season we will be touched more by Your presence than by our presents. In Jesus' name we pray. Amen.

Applying the Gift: Department stores will leave Christmas seekers smelling like mothballs, but Christ gives us the sweet, pure scent of heaven.

Wake From Your Sleep

2. Come from your fields as shepherds of old.
   Welcome this child whom prophets foretold.
   God has made the earth His home.
   Praise to our God the Savior has come.

3. Stay with us now, O Lord of the earth.
   Make of our hearts a place for Your birth.
   Though our cares be great or small.
   Jesus the Lord be born in us all.

Remain In His Love

JESUS CHRIST WAS ABLE to say at the end of His earthly life that He had obeyed God and therefore remained in His love. This gave Christ the joy which He then promised to us—complete joy in Him!

Following Christ is never dreary—we are challenged to take steps that involve risks. If we are obedient and take the steps, that alone is success! If we do not obey, we may miss opportunities that may never present themselves again.

Obedience assures us that we will learn lessons and, like Christ, accomplish the work God has given us to do (John 17: 4). If we refuse to let God use us, then we miss out on all the joy of being involved in accomplishing His plan.

Prayer:

How I praise Thee, precious Savior
That Thy love laid hold of me;
Thou hast saved and cleansed and filled me
That I might Thy channel be.

Channels only, blessed Master,
But with all Thy wondrous pow'r
Flowing through us, Thou can'st use us
Every day and every hour. *   Amen.

Applying the Gift: Christ is the only source of lasting love and joy. Believe that He will supply all the resources for all He asks you to do.

*From the hymn "Channels Only"

Remember This

Remember this, fix it in your mind, take it to heart, you rebels.

Remember the former things, those of long ago;

I am God, and there is no other;

I am God, and there is none like me.

I make known the end from the beginning,

> *from ancient times, what is still to come.*

I say: My purpose will stand, and I will do all that I please.

From the east I summon a bird of prey;

> *from a far-off land, a man to fulfill my purpose.*

What I have said, that will I bring about;

What I have planned, that will I do.

Listen to me...

Isaiah 46: 8–12a

G OD'S PROMISES ARE NEVER BROKEN—they are tokens of love for encouragement and hope, expressions of His mind and will. To be aware of them is to have a new understanding of the loving heart of God, our spiritual heritage and our destiny. They are waiting to be claimed; they challenge us to live holy lives.

The Old Testament is a history of a people and nation called by God. He revealed Himself to them over and over, always keeping His promises. But they doubted and disobeyed, falling into a pit of failure, fears, death and destruction until God intervened with the birth of Jesus.

All promises point to Jesus Christ, the Living Word of God. Paul says "For no matter how many promises God has made, they are 'Yes' in Christ. And so through Him, the 'Amen' is spoken by us to the glory of God," (II Corinthians 1:20) The nation Israel failed to recognize and understand Him, but do not let their failure become ours!

Prayer: "I heard the voice of Jesus say, 'I am this dark world's Light; Look unto Me, thy morn shall rise and all thy day be bright.' I looked to Jesus and I found in Him my Star, my Sun, And in that Light of Life I'll walk till traveling days are done"* Amen.

Applying the Gift: Remember this…a book of promises and a shining star point to Bethlehem, the Babe in a manger, and the glory of God. Ask yourself: "Have I fixed this in my mind and heart in a personal relationship with Jesus? If so, say "Amen" to the glory of God!

*Hymn–"I Heard the Voice of Jesus Say."
Text: Horatius Bonar

So whether you eat or drink or whatever you do, do it all for the glory of God.

I Corinthians 10:31

Be very careful, then, how you live—not as unwise but as wise, making the most of every opportunity, because the days are evil. Therefore do not be foolish, but understand what the Lord's will is.

Ephesians 5: 15–17

Tradition

A FEW YEARS AGO someone shared the following story with me which caused me to examine the traditions that I have followed for years.

A newlywed watched his wife one day while she was preparing dinner. He noticed that she cut the end off the ham before placing it in the pan. "Why do you do that, honey?"he asked her.

"Well, that's the way my mother always did it," she responded.

Sometime later he just happened to walk into his mother-in-law's kitchen just as she was cutting the end off the ham before placing it in the roaster. "Why do you do that?" he asked.

"I really don't know. It is just the way my mother always did it," she answered.

Grandma was in the next room, so he decided to try to solve the mystery. "Grandma, why do you cut the end off the ham before baking it?"

"I don't know why anyone else does it," she answered, "but I always did it because my pan was too small."

One of the Christmas traditions in my family when I was a child was to go pick out the most perfect evergreen tree we could find. That was a struggle because, as you know, no tree is perfect. After finding one most of us could agree on, we had it flocked with artificial snow. By the time the tree was flocked, the imperfections were hard to detect.

The tree reminds me of each one of us. We are all imperfect. "For all have sinned and fall short of the glory of God." (Romans 3:23)

The evergreen reminds me of our standing with Jesus as our Lord. "…that whoever believes in him shall not perish but have eternal life." (John 3:16b)

And the flocking reminds me of how we look to God after Jesus puts robes of righteousness on us after washing us in His blood. "Though your sins are like scarlet, they shall be as white as snow; though they are red as crimson, they shall be like wool." (Isaiah 1:18b)

Some traditions are good. I like many lights because Jesus is the only true light in a dark, sinful world. However, some traditions are meaningless to a Christian or may even have pagan origins. These can take away precious time and energy and can even make us tired and cross instead of loving.

Prayer: Heavenly Father, we desire to make our time count for You and Your kingdom, especially at the special times of the year when we honor You and what You have done. Please help us to make wise choices, for Your Word says that "If the Lord delights in a man's way, he makes his steps firm." (Psalm 37:23). Thank You for being so patient and merciful when we do wrong. We love You. In Jesus' Name.

Amen.

Applying the Gift: Meditate on the traditions which are time consumers. If they do not reflect God's glory or edify Him, let us dare to put them out of our lives. Perhaps this will give us more time to read the Bible, to pray, to visit a shut-in, or to do a kind deed.

Christmas Gift

I've been frantically running from store to store—
My shopping list grows—and demands more and more,
The house needs to be cleaned—the baking done
And there's not enough hours under the sun—to do it all.
I'm tired and irritable and there's no time I can see
To polish the silver and trim the tree.

I'm finally home—the shopping's done.
I've unloaded the packages—one by one
And, thank heaven there are no more—
Then, I pause for breath—just outside the door.

It is a still and starlit night
And there is one star that is very bright.
I look around at the mountains and trees
And a sense of peace steals over me.

Suddenly, there are Judean hills
And the night is cold and white and still.
I can hear the murmur of the sheep
As they settle down for a night of sleep.

Shepherds pull their robes round their shoulders—tight
Against the chill of the winter night.
The fire in its nest of rock
Crackles a background to their talk.

I move closer and strain to hear
The excited voices huddled near.
"It's still like a dream," I hear one sigh.
"But the Babe was there!" comes the quick reply.
"Why should we be the ones to hear! Why me!
A priest, perhaps, or even a Rabbi,
But why someone as humble as I!"

The wind whispers gently—a car door slams—
And I remember where I am.
Oh yes, Dear Father—Oh yes, why me?
Others are worthier, you can see—
But you chose to show me your glory bright!
Dear Father, I thank You for Christ tonight.

Lois Watts

Peace

Do not be anxious about anything, but in everything, by prayer and petition, with thanksgiving, present your requests to God. And the peace of God, which transcends all understanding, will guard your hearts and your minds in Christ Jesus.

Philippians 4: 6, 7

IN DECEMBER AND AS CHRISTMAS NEARS, my thoughts of peace are renewed and revitalized. On Christmas Day, the day we celebrate the birth of our Savior Jesus Christ, my thoughts turn to what the birth of the baby Jesus has meant in my life. He brought me peace, and this has brought so much harmony and tranquility to my life.

He not only came into this world to die for me, giving me the promise of eternal life, but He has brought peace into my life while here on earth. To illustrate this, I would like to share a personal testimony.

My husband and I have both been through life-threatening diseases. We have lost a child in a tragic death. We have been through divorce with our children. We have lost dear relatives and friends through tragedy and untimely death. These are a few of the major incidents we have experienced, but through it all God has supplied us with a peace that is beyond our understanding.

Let me list a few of our favorite verses that helped us through these times:

Romans 8:26 through 28 says that in the midst of your burden when you know not how to pray, the spirit "intercedes…in accordance with God's will." The peace you experience from knowing this is truly amazing.

Isaiah 41:10 and 13 states that when you know He is upholding you with His righteous right hand, the peace you experience is beyond description.

Luke 2:11, I John 4:14 and John 3:16 verify that He came into this world to die for us, take our sins upon Himself and give us eternal life. Truly He is the Prince of Peace.

You might like to look up a few more favorite verses on peace: they are Isaiah 26:3, John 14:27, John 16:33 and Psalm 4:8.

Prayer: Father, I want to experience this peace that only You can give. I want You to come into my heart and life and be my Savior. Amen.

Applying the Gift: Peace floods the soul when Christ rules the heart.

Jesus Christ Is Born

In those days Caesar Augustus issued a decree that a census should be taken of the entire Roman world. (This was the first census that took place while Quirinius was governor of Syria.) And everyone went to his own town to register.

So Joseph also went up from the town of Nazareth in Galilee to Judea, to Beth-lehem the town of David, because he belonged to the house and line of David. He went there to register with Mary, who was pledged to be married to him and was expecting a child. While they were there, the time came for the baby to be born, and she gave birth to her firstborn, a son. She wrapped him in cloths and placed him in a manger, because there was no room for them in the inn.

Luke 2: 1–7

Look up and see the Christmas Star
That leads to Bethlehem,
And find the baby Jesus
Born to take away our sin.

The road that leads to Bethlehem
It really isn't far.
Look! I see some shepherds.
Have you seen the star?

Let's walk a little faster
It surely can't be far,
Here come some wise men from the East.
Have you seen the star?

We reach the town of Bethlehem
The angels light our way,
We've found the baby Jesus
Upon a bed of hay.

Yes, we found the baby Jesus
There is no need to look far,
Just look for Him within your heart
And you will see His Star.

Prayer: May God bless you and surround you with His love this blessed season and through the coming year. Amen.

Applying the Gift: We search for the Child diligently: let us search for the Man.

Hallelujah! Christmas Music!

How beautiful on the mountains
*   are the feet of those who bring good*
*   news,*
who proclaim peace,
*   who bring good tidings,*
*   who proclaim salvation,*
who say to Zion,
*   "Your God reigns!"*
Listen! Your watchmen lift up their
*   voices;*
*   together they shout for joy.*
When the Lord returns to Zion,
*   they will see it with their own eyes.*
Burst into songs of joy together,
*   you ruins of Jerusalem,*
for the Lord has comforted his people,
*   he has redeemed Jerusalem.*
The Lord will lay bare his holy arm
*   in the sight of all the nations,*
and all the ends of the earth will see
*   the salvation of our God.*
*   Isaiah 52:7–10*

Music helps us prepare for Christmas. Among our Christmas records and tapes, most of us will find a copy of Handel's great oratorio "Messiah", which includes the "Hallelujah Chorus."

George Frideric Handel, composer of the oratorio, helps us to "prepare the way." The source of his inspiration was Jesus Christ. Handel knew the Wonderful Counselor of whom he wrote. Because he composed his oratorio in only three weeks, the ink at the top of the page would still be wet when he reached the bottom of the page. His oratorio was first presented in Dublin, Ireland, and he gave the receipts to care for orphans, the sick, and prisoners. Handel said that he had been a sick man whom God had cured and that he had been a prisoner but had been set free. In his "Messiah" he surely helped all who have heard the music to prepare for Christmas.

Thanks be to God for inspired music and for Christ, the source of our inspiration.

Prayer: Heavenly Father, help us as we prepare our hearts to celebrate Christ's birth. Strengthen us with inspired words of song as we continue our journey to Bethlehem. Amen.

Applying the Gift: "Praise ye the Lord. Sing unto the Lord a new song." (Psalm 149:1)

"...for music is a gift of God, not an invention of man."
*   Martin Luther*

Those Were The Good Ole Days?

Joy... Why would the week before Christmas be called the joy week? Wouldn't you think that the week in which Jesus arrived would be the week we celebrate with joy? If you remember, however, the words "joy" and "anticipation" are often linked when we speak of Christmas.

Maybe this is because joy can be defined, as C.S. Lewis does, as the delight we feel in anticipation. Think of children as they anticipate Christmas. Often they feel more joy as they wait for Christmas, eagerly shaking the packages and trying to find out what's inside of them, than they do after they have opened all the presents and the living room is a tornado of wrapping paper and bows. Think, too, of the last time you read a really good book—the kind you "can't put down." Weren't you inspired, as you read, by a longing and deep desire to experience what was in the novel? And what brought about this feeling the most? It wasn't in the completion of the book, was it? No, this kind of joy welled up in your heart as you turned each and every last page, seeking to experience what was happening in the book.

I think Christ would have us live our lives with this kind of joy. Many of us live life in unhappy anticipation of when we will *really* have joy—when we get a good job, that next promotion comes, or we can retire; when the summer holidays come or we graduate; when we marry, our toddler learns to walk, or our kids leave home; when the weather is not quite so hot, or cold, or rainy; when the church has more members, or programs, or money; when we lose weight, or gain it, or learn to maintain it; when our spiritual life is on the upswing again, we've won ten souls to Christ, or Christ returns. Goals are important to strive for. If we did not set them we might not accomplish anything—but we must remember that often the joy is in the anticipation of the goal, as well as the attainment thereof.

Prayer: Dear God, please help us to feel the joy of anticipation in our everyday lives. Give us eyes that can see the special parts of each stage of our lives. When we believe that we are in God's will, teach us, as Jim Elliott suggests, to live each moment to the fullest. Amen.

Applying the Gift: When you look back on this time of your life, what things are you going to remember that will prompt you to say, "Ah, yes, those were the good ole days"? Why not cherish them today?

Do not say, "Why were the old days bet-
*   ter than these?"*
For it is not wise to ask such questions.
When times are good, be happy;
*   but when times are bad, consider:*
God has made the one as well as the
*   other.*
Therefore, a man cannot discover any-
*   thing about his future.*
*   Ecclesiastes 7:10, 14*

Guard your Vision jealously,
It is attainable
Take your yearning seriously
It is the presence of God in you.

Gather strength
**   when all growth is frozen**
**   and then burst forth**
**   to let your vision grow again.**

Color it, give it substance
Point yourself into its center
**   where you belong.**
Be at home with yourself. God is.
**   —Anonymous**

The Building Of A Family

IT WAS CHRISTMAS 1979. Our marriage was twenty-seven years old. Our six children ranged in age from twenty-six to sixteen, and they were all home for Christmas.

Our family had celebrated many Christmases together. The first, for my husband and me, was a snowy Christmas, twelve days after our wedding. We were both college students, living in a small apartment. Our tiny Christmas tree, the gift of an aunt, sat on a desk dwarfed by the simple gifts we had for each other. That Christmas our gifts reflected the needs of our new home: a frying pan, an alarm clock, and a popcorn popper.

A few years later, Christmas found us in sunny California, and our tree was on an enclosed porch. We had spread warm blankets on the linoleum floor to ward off the morning chill. Five of us opened our treasures: a doll for sister, a set of blocks for baby brother, a toy earthmover, called a "humdinger" for big brother, a new saw for Dad, and a blouse for me.

Christmas 1979 was a time of celebration and anticipation. More years had passed, and now we were eight; in fact, even more. Two of our children had married and two others would marry within months. Except for our last teenager, all were adults now, pursuing adult lives.

We had worshipped by candlelight on Christmas Even, singing the beautiful old carols, hearing God's words and attending the Lord's table. Morning found the big tree in our living room with too many gifts to fit under the branches. One son played "Santa Claus," distributing flannel shirts, pretty sweaters, towels for the new households, decorated cans of carmel corn and cookies, and calendars for the New Year. We tried to be organized, but bright paper was everywhere and socks lost their mates. Somehow, all the "sticky" bows seemed to land on my hair, producing a bright Christmas cap.

Later, after our traditional dinner, we spilled outdoors into the sunny afternoon. It was time to take pictures: the original two, the six grown offspring, the "in-laws" and the "out-laws," those who would soon join our family. Our six even posed to duplicate a picture taken ten years earlier, dressing, combing and trying to make the same "faces."

This was a Christmas when God's provision included both fulfillment and promise. God had been with us through many years as our marriage was maturing and our children growing to adulthood: the years had seen asthma and chickenpox, report cards, school plays, music lessons and choir rehearsals; learning to sew, cook and drive; and learning to think ahead and make decisions. With God's provision, there had been baptisms, confessions of faith, and church membership. My husband and I had great satisfaction in the "big" job of our lives nearly accomplished.

We looked ahead with anticipation. Already new "twos" were joining their lives together, establishing new homes where God would be honored, where children would come–in God's time. There would be new times for the two of us, putting more leaves in the table at holiday dinners, advising our offspring at their request, and having more time for each other. There would be trips to visit our families moved away, new adventures and new challenges.

In all of our future life, God would be faithful just as He always had. The cycle of our family was beginning again.

Prayer: Almighty God, we praise You for Your faithfulness through all the times of our lives and families. Help us realize that You hold eternal plans for us as You guide us in the small steps that accomplish them. We trust You for each day. In Jesus' Name. Amen.

Applying the Gift: List provisions in your life that only God could have given. Let these build your confidence for days ahead.

Joy Is Ours For The Taking

"I am the true vine, and my Father is the gardener. He cuts off every branch in me that bears no fruit, while every branch that does bear fruit he prunes so that it will be even more fruitful. You are already clean because of the word I have spoken to you. Remain in me, and I will remain in you. No branch can bear fruit by itself; it must remain in the vine. Neither can you bear fruit unless you remain in me.

"I am the vine; you are the branches. If a man remains in me and I in him, he will bear much fruit; apart from me you can do nothing. If anyone does not remain in me, he is like a branch that is thrown away and withers; such branches are picked up, thrown into the fire and burned. If you remain me and my words remain in you, ask whatever you wish, and it will be given you. This is to my Father's glory, that you bear much fruit, showing yourselves to be my disciples.

"As the Father has loved me, so have I loved you. Now remain in my love. If you obey my commands, you will remain in my love, just as I have obeyed my Father's commands and remain in his love. I have told you this so that my joy may be in you and that your joy may be complete."

John 15: 1–11

The Christmas season is a time of Joy. Everyone remembers this time of the year with happy memories—whether it be singing Christmas carols, lighting advent candles, eating goodies, sharing with our families, or just listening to the Christmas story. It is wonderful to remember what God gave us on that first Christmas so long ago and we wonder what kind of gift we can give to Him in return.

All that the Lord asks of us is that we abide in Him. Jesus told us that if we keep the commandments, we will abide in God's love. When we think about all that God has given us—the earth, our food, our lives, His love, and even His Son—is it too much to ask of us that we keep His commandments? All we have to do is follow some very simple rules, which are exactly what the commandments are, and abide in Him. The Lord says that if we abide in Him, and His words in us, we may ask whatever we will and it will be done for us. How can we refuse?

There are times when keeping the commandments does not seem so simple. We say it is okay to tell someone a little "white" lie and it is all right to steal somebody's pen if he has another one just like it. There are times, too, when we feel as if that mean, unfriendly neighbor got what he deserved when someone tore up his yard. We can add other commandment-breakers to our list, but when we realize we are failing to keep His commandments, all we need to do is turn back to God. His arms are big enough to carry all our loads. If we feel temptation knocking at our door, we can go to God in prayer because His ears are always open.

In John 15:11, Jesus said, "I have told you this so that my joy may be in you and that your joy may be complete."

Prayer: Dear Heavenly Father, we know that for all the joy You have given us, You ask only that we abide in You. Lord, give us the strength to follow Your commandments so that we will know Joy every minute of every day. Amen.

Applying the Gift: If we abide in Him our Joy will be full!

Do you not know?
  Have you not heard?
Has it not been told you from the beginning?
  Have you not understood since the earth was founded?
He sits enthroned above the circle of the earth,
  and its people are like grasshoppers.
He stretches out the heavens like a canopy,
  and spreads them out like a tent to live in.
He brings princes to naught
  and reduces the rulers of this world to nothing.
No sooner are they planted,
  no sooner are they sown,
  no sooner do they take root in the ground,
than he blows on them and they wither,
  and a whirlwind sweeps them away like chaff.

To whom will you compare me?
  Or who is my equal?" says the Holy One.
Lift your eyes and look to the heavens:
  Who created all these?
He who brings out the starry host one by one,
  and calls them each by name.

Because of his great power and mighty strength,
  not one of them is missing.

Why do you say, O Jacob,
  and complain, O Israel,
"My way is hidden from the Lord;
  my cause is disregarded by my God"?
Do you not know?
  Have you not heard?
The Lord is the everlasting God,
  the Creator of the ends of the earth.
He will not grow tired or weary,
  and his understanding no one can fathom.
He gives strength to the weary
  and increases the power of the weak.
Even youths grow tired and weary.
  and young men stumble and fall;
but those who hope in the Lord
  will renew their strength.
They will soar on wings like eagles;
  they will run and not grow weary,
  they will walk and not be faint.

Isaiah 40: 21–31

Our Names Are Known

ONE OF THE SUREST WAYS to win friends and influence people is to learn the names of individuals, and to know what they like to be called in any given situation. With some people the appellation of Mr. or Ms. seems overly formal in a situation, but others would rather not have you call them by their given name unless you were a very close friend.

Names are important; it has been said that the sweetest sound to a person's ear is the calling of his or her own name. It even sounds better if we hear our name called by someone important.

He who created the starry host calls each one by name. Not one of them is missing, and not one star is forgotten. A bit of poetry refers to stars as "dead and inanimate." This should give living and breathing human beings great joy for if we consider the biblical fact that God knows each star by name–and Scripture tells us they are numbered with the sands of the seashore–how much more then can we expect Him to know our names, for we have been created in His image! May we take great joy during this Advent season in knowing that God knows us and calls us by name!

Prayer: O God who knows us, help us to know You. Amen.

Applying the Gift: Because of His great power and strength, not one of us will be missing.

The Season of the Secret

What I am saying is that as long as the heir is a child, he is no different from a slave, although he owns the whole estate. He is subject to guardians and trustees until the time set by his father. So also, when we were children, we were in slavery under the basic principles of the world. But when the time had fully come, God sent his Son, born of a woman, born under law, to redeem those under law, that we might receive the full rights of sons. Because you are sons, God sent the Spirit of his Son into our hearts, the Spirit who calls out, "Abba, Father." So you are no longer a slave, but a son; and since you are a son, God has made you also an heir.

Galatians 4: 1–7

In Silence

At Christmas time the world I see
Is filled with reverent ecstasy
And silence fills the countryside
Across the fields flung far and wide
Where not a bit of earth can show
For all is deep and white with snow.

At evening time I search afar
To see the shining Christmas Star
In silence calling us to come
To praise and worship God's dear
   *Son.**

George L. Ehrman

Used by permission from *Living Values*, published by Good News Publishers, Westchester, IL 60153

CHRISTMAS IS OFTEN CALLED the season of gift-giving. Think of it also as the season of secrets.

Before a gift is given, we prepare for the right moment to share our tokens of love. We choose and wrap our presents and hide them behind closed doors or on closet shelves. These Christmas secrets, however, are not planned to be permanent. When the proper moment arrives, we share our secrets with laughter, smiles, and surprise.

God had a secret about His Word which was with him from the beginning. He spoke of it through prophets, priests, and wise men. "When the time had fully come, God sent forth His Son." His secret was the gift of Jesus Christ. What a token of love!

Receiving this gift can make this the happiest Christmas ever!

Prayer: Heavenly Father, thank You for Your saving gift of Jesus and help us to share your gift with family, friends, and all the people we meet along life's way. Amen.

Applying the Gift: The Joy we have over Christ's birth depends on our preparation for His coming.

Y{\scriptsize EARS AGO SOME UNKNOWN WRITER}, speaking of the influence of Jesus through nineteen hundred years of Christian history, said:

"Here is a man who was born in an obscure village
    the child of a peasant woman.
He grew up in another village, and that a despised one.
He worked in a carpenter shop for thirty years,
    and then for three years He was an itinerant preacher.
He never wrote a book.
He never held an office.
He never owned a home.
He never had a family.
He never went to college.
He never put His foot inside a really big city.
He never traveled, except in His infancy,
    more than two hundred miles from the place where He was born.
He had no credentials but HIMSELF.

"While still a young man,
    The tide of popular opinion turned against Him.
His friends ran away.
One of them betrayed Him.
He was turned over to His enemies.
He went through the mockery of a trial.
He was nailed upon a Cross between two thieves.
His executors gambled for the only piece of property
    He had on earth, His seamless robe.
When He was dead,
    He was taken down from the cross and laid in a borrowed grave through the courtesy of a friend.
Nineteen wide centuries have come and gone,
    and today Jesus is the centerpiece of the human race,
    and the leader of all human progress.

"I am well within the mark when I say that all the armies that ever marched,
    all the navies that were ever built, all the parliaments that have ever sat, and
    all the kings that have ever ruled put together have not affected the life of man upon this earth like this one solitary personality.

"All time dates from his birth, and it is impossible to understand or interpret the progress of human civilization in any nation on earth apart from his influence. Slowly through the ages man is coming to realize that the greatest necessity in the world is not water, iron, gold, food and clothing, or even nitrate in the soil; but rather Christ enshrined in human hearts, thoughts and motives.

"More poems have been written, more stories told, more pictures painted, and more songs sung about Christ than any other person in human history, because through such avenues as these the deepest appreciation of the human heart can be more adequately expressed."

The Birth of Jesus

Angels played a very important
part in the birth of Jesus.
The angel, Gabriel, told Mary that
she was going to have a baby and
that his name would be Jesus. The angels
told the wise men and the shepherds
that a new king was being
born in Bethlehem.

Baby Jesus was born in Bethlehem
to Mary and Joseph. The wise
men brought Jesus gold, frankincense
and myrrh.

Jesus died for our sins,
rose again, and ascended
into heaven.

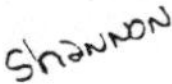

God Really Loves You

For God so loved the world that he gave his one and only Son, that whoever believes in him shall not perish but have eternal life.

John 3:16

Jesus said to her, "I am the resurrection and the life. He who believes in me will live, even though he dies; and whoever lives and believes in me will never die. Do you believe this?"

John 11:25–26

Jesus answered, "I am the way and the truth and the life. No one comes to the Father except through me. If you really knew me, you would know my Father as well. From now on, you do know him and have seen him."

John 14:6

Jesus said, "But I, when I am lifted up from the earth, will draw all men to myself."

John 12:32

How can a person who does not know God personally come to know that God does exist and that He truly loves that person? Knowing God's love can lead to a life filled with peace and assurance that cannot be experienced apart from Him.

The Bible, God's inspired Word to humankind, describes God as the One who created the universe, the planet Earth and the creatures who live on Earth (Genesis 1–2). The Bible tells how God revealed Himself to humans and showed His love to the people He made. The ultimate expression of His love was in His visiting Earth as a human being in the person of Jesus Christ. Jesus lived among humans and taught them the ways of God. He showed people the grace of God through the forgiveness of sins and the healing of diseases.

Jesus' death on the Cross of Calvary and His resurrection three days later have allowed people to have eternal reconciliation with God through the forgiveness of their sins. Before Christ, people sought God's forgiveness by offering repeated sacrifices, with a lamb's blood atoning for the people's sins. Christ's sacrifice on the Cross ended that need for animal sacrifices. Jesus took upon Himself the sins of everyone and invited all people to trust in Him as their Savior.

If you believe that Jesus Christ died so that you could have a right relationship with God, please ask God in prayer to wash your sins away so that you may have the assurance of eternal life. Then you will know how much God really loves you!

神は本当にあなたを愛していらっしゃいます

ヨハネ　3：16ーー神は、実に、そのひとり子をお与えになったほどに、世を愛された。それは御子を信じるものが、ひとりとして滅びることなく、永遠のいのちを持つためである。

ヨハネ　11：25ー26ーーイエスは言われた。「わたしは、よみがえりです。いのちです。わたしを信じる者は、死んでも生きるのです。また、生きていてわたしを信じる者は、決して死ぬことがありません。このことを信じますか。」

ヨハネ　14：6ー7ーーイエスは彼に言われた。「わたしが道であり、真理であり、いのちなのです。わたしを通してでなければ、だれひとり父のみもとに来ることはありません。あなたがたは、もしわたしを知っていたなら父をも知っていたはずです。しかし、今や、あなたがたは父を知っており、また、すでに父を見たのです。」

ヨハネ12：32ーーイエスは言われた。「わたしが地上から上げられるなら、わたしはすべての人を自分のところに引き寄せます。」

　神を個人的に知らない人が、神は実際に存在し、その人を本当に愛しているということを知るにはどのようにすればよいでしょうか？　わたしたちは神の愛を知ると、神から離れていては知ることのできない、平安と確かさのある人生へと導かれることができます。

　神の霊感によって人類に語られた、神の言葉である聖書は、神を宇宙、地球という惑星、また地球上に住む生物を創造された方であるといっています。　聖書は、神がどのようにご自分のお造りになった人間にご自身を現わし、愛を示されたかということをわたしたちに伝えています。　そして、神の愛の究極の表現は、この地球上にイエス・キリストが人となっておとずれたことでした。

　イエス・キリストは人間の間に住み、神の道を説きました。彼は罪を許し、病を癒すことを通して神の恵みを人々に示しました。

　カルバリの丘でイエスが十字架上で死なれ、三日後によみがえられたことによって、わたしたちは罪を許され、神と永遠に和解することができました。　キリストが現れる前までは、人々はいけにえを繰り返し捧げることで神のゆるしを求め、仔羊の血によって罪をあがなっていました。　キリストの十字架上での犠牲は、この動物のいけにえをなくしました。

　イエスは全ての人の罪を負い、全ての人が自分を救い主として信じるように招かれました。

　イエス・キリストは、あなたが神と正しい関係を持てるように死んだということをもし信じるなら、祈りによって、あなたの罪をあらいきよめ、永遠の命の確信を持てるように神に求めてください。　そうすれば神がどれほどあなたのことを愛しているか知ることができます。

約翰福音 3:16
"神愛世人甚至將他的獨生子賜給他們，叫一切信他仍不至滅亡，反得永生."

約翰福音 11:25-26
耶穌對他說:"復活在我，生命也在我，信我的人，雖然死了，也必復活. 凡活著信我的人，必永遠不死. 你信這話麼."

約翰福音 14:6-7
耶穌說:"我就是道路真理生命，若不藉著我，沒有人能到父那裡去，你們若認識我，也就認識我的父. 從今以後，你們認識他，並且已經看見他."

約翰福音 12:32
"我若從地上被舉起來，就要吸引萬人來歸我."

怎樣才可以帶領一個不認識神的人去相信神的存在和瞭解他的愛呢? 能夠明白神的愛是可以使生命充滿和平和滿足

聖經是由神的聖靈感動所啟示而寫出來的一本書，它的內容是描述這位創造宇宙，天地萬物的主宰(創世記1-2章). 聖經告訴我們神顯現他自己在世人面前，並表達他對我們的愛，他將自己的兒子，耶穌，道成肉身來到世上，就是叫他教導我們神的旨意，神的恩典就利用耶穌在世上的時候，施予世人，赦免世人的罪和醫治世人的病痛.

耶穌被釘死在十字架上所流出的血和三天後的復活都使我們罪人和神得以和好. 在主耶穌基督出生前，世人都獻上羊的血作祭品來祈求神的寬恕. 但在主耶穌基督死後，他的血已將我們過去，現在和未來的罪全都洗清. 他已經使我們在神面前得到完全的寬恕.

如果你相信主耶穌基督已為你釘在十字架上，洗清你的罪，使你能和神有甜美關係的時候. 請你現在誠心祈禱，開啟你的心，懇求神的赦免和接納，他會賜予你有永恆的生命，更加可以令你感受他甜美的愛.

¡Dios Te Ama, Sin Duda!

*orque de tal manera amó Dios al
*aundo qúe ha dado a su Hijo
*nigénito, para que todo aquel que en
*l cree, no se pierda mas tenga vida
terna.

Juan 3:16

*e dijo Jesús: Yo soy la resurrección
*la vida; el que cree en mí, aunque
*sté muerto, va a vivir. Y todo aquel
*ue vive y cree en mí, no va a morir
ternamente. ¿Crees esto?

Juan 11:25–26

*Y yo, si fuere levantado de la tierra, a
odos voy a atraer a mí mismo.

Juan 12:32

*esús le dijo: Yo soy el camino, y la
*erdad, y la vida; nadie viene al Pa-
re, sino por mí.

Juan 14:6

¿COMO SE PUEDE SABER, sin duda, que Dios existe y que este Dios ama a cada persona, sin conocer a este Dios personalmente? Una conocimiento del amor de Dios va a resultar en una vida llena de la paz y la seguridad que no se puede ser experimentado aparte de Él.

La Biblia, la Palabra inspirida por Dios que ha dado El a la humanidad, describe a Dios como El que creó los cielos, la Tierra y todas las criaturas que en él la vive. La Biblia nos dice que Dios nos ha revelado a sí mismo y nos ha demonstrado su amor que tiene Él para su creacion. El exemplo de este amor más grande se puede ver cuando Dios visitó al mundo como ser humano, en la persona de Jesucristo. Jesús vivió entre la humanidad y les enseñó las maneras de Dios. Les mostró la gracia de Dios por la perdón de los pecados y por curar las enfermedades de la gente.

La muerte de Jesucristo en la Cruz a Calvario y su resurrección dentro de tres dias ha hecho posible reconciliación entre Dios y la humanidad porque Jesucristo ha ofrecido a sí mismo en nuestro lugar en pagamiento por todos los pecados del mundo. Antes de Cristo, la gente de Dios trataba de obtener perdón por ofrecer sacrificios de la sangre de animales para compensación por sus pecados. El sacrificio de Jesucristo ha puesto fin a este tipo de sacrificio, porque Él sufrió la pena por los pecados del mundo. Este Jesús mismo invita a todo el mundo confiar en El como su Salvador.

Si crees tú que Jesucristo se murió para que puedas tener una relación personal con Dios, favor de pedir a Dios en oración que el quite tus pecados y darte la seguridad que tienes vida eterna. ¡Si hagas eso, vas a comprender de tal manera Dios te ama!

Wahrlich. Gott liebt dich.

Also hat Gott die Welt geliebt, daß Er Seinen eingeborenen Sohn gab, auf daß alle, die an Ihn glauben, nicht verloren werden, sondern das ewige Leben haben.

Johannes 3:16

Jesus spricht zu ihr: Ich bin die Auferstehung und das Leben. Wer an mich glaubt, der wird leben, ob er gleich stürbe; und wer da lebt und glaubt an mich, der wird nimmermehr sterben. Glaubst du das?

Johannes 11:25–26

Jesus sprich zu ihm: ,,Ich bin der Weg und die Wahrheit und das Leben; niemand kommt zum Vater denn durch mich. Wenn ihr mich kennt, so kennt ihr auch meinen Vater. Und von nun an kennt ihr Ihn und habt Ihn gesehen.''

Johannes 14:6–7

Jesus spricht: ,, Und ich, wenn ich erhöht werde von der Erde, so will ich sie alle zu mir ziehen.''

Johannes 12:32

WIE KANN DER MENSCH, der nicht an Gott glaubt, zur Kenntnis kommen daß Gott existiert und daß Gott den Menschen wahrlich liebt? Die kenntnis der Liebe Gottes kann dazu führen, daß das Leben voll Frieden und Zuversicht ist, aber ohne Gott kann man das nicht erfahren.

Die Bibel ist Gottes Wort an die Menschheit. Gott wird darin als Schöpfer des Weltraumes, der Erde und aller Kreaturen die auf Erden leben beschrieben (Das Buch Mose 1-2). Die Bibel erklärt wie Gott sich den Menschen offenbart und wie Er seine Liebe den Menschen, die Er schuf, beweist. Der größte Beweis Seiner Liebe bestand in Seinen Wanderungen auf Erden in der Gestalt Jesus Christus. Jesus lebte unter den Menschen und brachte ihnen Gottes Wege bei. Durch das Vergeben der Sünden und Heilen der Kranken zeigte Jesus den Menschen Gottes Gnade.

Jesus Tod am Kreuz zu Golgatha und Sein Auferstehen drei Tage später, ermöglicht den Menschen eine ewige Versöhnung mit Gott durch das Vergeben der Sünden zu erziehlen. Vor Christus suchten die Menschen Gottes Vergebung durch das wiederholte Darbringen von Opfern, und mit dem Blut des Lammes versuchten sie für die Sünden zu büßen. Mit Christus Opfer am Kreuz fand das Opfern der Tiere ein Ende. Jesus nahm die Sünden aller Menschen auf seine Schultern und er ladet alle ein Ihm als Retter zu trauen.

Wenn du glaubst, daß Jesus Christus starb, um dir ein richtiges Verhältnis mit Gott zu ermöglichen, dann sollst du Gott im Gebet bitten daß er deine Sünden wegwäscht und daß du auch Zuversicht auf ein ewiges Leben haben kannst. Dann wirst du wirklich wissen wie sehr dich Gott liebt.

I Heard the Bells
On Christmas Day

I heard the bells on Christmas day
Their old familiar carols play,
and wild and sweet the words repeat
of peace on earth, goodwill to men.

I thought how, as the day had come,
The belfries of all Christendom
Had rolled along th' unbroken song
Of peace on earth, goodwill to men.

And in despair I bowed my head;
"There is no peace on earth," I said,
"For hate is strong, and mocks the
  song
Of peace on earth, goodwill to men."

Then pealed the bells more loud and
  deep:
"God is not dead, nor doth He sleep:
The wrong shall fail, the right
  prevail,
With peace on earth, goodwill to
  men."

Till, ringing, singing on its way,
The world revolved from night to
  day,
A voice, a chime, a chant sublime,
Of peace on earth, goodwill to men!
   Henry Wadsworth Longfellow

"Peace On Earth, Good Will To Men"

THERE ARE SLEIGH BELLS, silver bells, wedding bells, church bells, bells "on her toes," and Poe's silver, gold, bronze and iron bells (symbolizing the four ages of man or stages in life). But the best bells of all are the bells of Christmas Day. Longfellow aptly used these Christmas bells when he wrote the words to the only genuine "Christ"mas carol by a writer from the United States.

In the first stanza the bells ring out "wild and sweet," suggesting a return to the wildness of a perfect nature. The message is so familiar that we often forget to think about the words of the carols; and in this stanza, "peace on earth, good will to men" seems to be a nice meaningless platitude.

In the second stanza the poet muses on how the Christian religion has become world-wide and how, if we could follow the sounds of Christmas bells from continent to continent, the song would be ringing wherever Christ's church appears on earth.

However, in the third stanza the poet contemplates the meaning of the words "peace on earth, good will to men" and juxtaposes the thought against the reality of hate and continual warfare. He is led to despair and goes so far as to say that the hate on earth makes the words of that song a mockery. How often we are inclined to agree with him when we see what man has done to fellow man!

The fourth stanza shows that the bells will not be silenced; they persevere and become louder and deeper. The Christmas bells almost chastise the thoughts of the poet when they peal that "God is not dead, nor doth he sleep." Some years ago the philosopher Nietzsche theorized that God was dead, and the theory became quite popular among unbelievers and the avant-garde. However, if God thinks about Nietzsche at all, he could well comment that "Nietzsche is dead." Who thinks very often about Nietzsche? But no dead God could live in the hearts of so many. Also, the idea of a sleeping God reminds me of the story of Elijah as he derided the prophets of Baal, saying that Baal must be asleep or, perhaps, on a journey. The ineffectiveness of false gods who cannot answer prayers clearly shows in this episode. In some ways, I believe we are all like those prophets, honoring money and success. However, the poet does not end on a negative note, even in this stanza. He assures us that, in the end, the right shall prevail.

The joyous final stanza has the bells ringing, singing, and chiming. They are not clashing and clanging with dissonance; in fact, they are not even pealing. There are no harsh sounds in this stanza, but only the promise of day and the sublime chant of "peace on earth, good will to men."

Prayer: Dear Father, help us to celebrate and vibrate the joy that only You can bring. Thank You for Your Son. Amen.

Applying the Gift: When hope is gone, and despair raises its ugly head, remember the message of the angels.

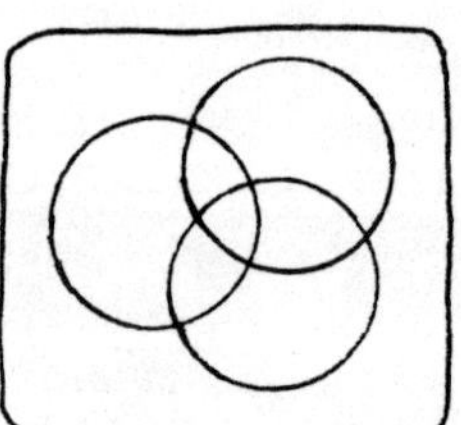

The Best Gift Of All

WHILE A CANCER PATIENT one December, my bodily functions went out of sync, depositing me in a reclining position; and I was afforded a blessed opportunity to "look up" many times. Common noises were unbearable, so I stuffed cotton in my ears to drown out the drone. Though lazy eyelids flopped down constantly, the mind was awake and busy.

In this forced solitude, I found myself listening to the "still, small voice within." It softly nudged my consciousness into a new awareness of the real meaning of Christmas. Since I was not able to "do" Christmas for my family of five young adult children, I wrote them the following Christmas letter:

MY CHRISTMAS GIFT TO YOU

Remember that year when at a Cub Scout Pack Christmas party some of you older ones thought your four-year-old sister was pretty dumb not to see that the wonderful Santa there was really her own dad? Well, there have been times when we have all failed to recognize the real man under the outer trappings. Let us take a good look at your father.

There has not been any man who has loved his family more than this man has—as much, perhaps, but not more. I remember back to each birth, how excited he always was! His babies were the greatest—the cutest, strongest, smartest. They were his.

His energies always have poured into providing for his own. But his love was so total, so unconditional. Do you know any man who loves his wife more completely, more blindly, than he? His love for me just "blows my mind"! He picked me, you know. I did not exactly go for him right at first. But you know how he is when he finds something he wants—he just methodically, without fanfare and also without much delay, sees that he gets it!

Then, rapidly, the wonderful babies came. How he loved it! There was never any shadow of an idea that another baby would be "too much"; and he helped with their care back then when it was not nearly so "in." He even changed messy diapers—the old-fashioned kind you had to rinse out and use over again, and again, and again.

Nobody could soothe a fussy baby the way he could—absolutely nobody. And he was happy to take his kids with him when he went places. They could go with him anywhere he needed to be. They were his, and special. When his young progeny were totally dependent on a parent-figure for all their needs, he was always meeting those needs, lovingly and generously.

As the years changed, the needs of his precious brood changed and they grew less dependent on the parent-figure. Heartaches, disappointments, fears and doubts entered into the relationship. Sometimes that is how it is as human beings change from babies to adolescents. Misunderstandings, antagonisms, accusations, guilts, un-loving acts, hostile attitudes—these can become a part of the father-child relationship, coming from and directed toward each side of the "generation gap." But the love—the constant, unfailing love cannot be quenched. In all situations, this is his family, the most precious people anywhere who continue to get his total attention and commitment.

He is human and not perfect, and his mistakes intermingle with the short-comings of others. At times, there are both physical and emotional separation between the man and his child, but the love keeps on and stays, and stays.

Remember all the wonderful times of teaching, sharing, caring, and fun? If one of us needs this guy, we know where to find him; he is always going to be home when his workday ends. Anyone can keep in touch if the desire or need is there.

Now we have all grown older, and still there is this love that just keeps on deepening. We take advantage of Dad—his time, his material goods, his wisdom, and his knowledge, but, most of all, of his goodness and of his love that "just won't quit."

And that is what Christmas is all about—a father's love that "just won't quit."

The greatest gift of all, you already have—the example of your dad who, with the rest of us, is made in the image and likeness of God. When you look at the kind of father-love demonstrated by such a man, an erring human…

…take the next step.

Consider the identity of your perfect Father, the Creator.
Romans 8:16–Galatians 3:26

Know how much God loves us, no matter how often our worldly life and affairs, our attitudes and behavior are contrary to His commands.
Romans 5:8–Luke 15:7

Dare to let your mind comprehend how special you are to the Lord God.
Jeremiah 31:3–Luke 15:10

Luxuriate in the bountiful supply of resources your Perfect Father has from which to bestow good things upon you.
Matthew 7:7–11

Thank God for the unspeakable gift of His son, Jesus…
II Corinthians 5:21–John 3:16

…and have yourself a VERY MERRY CHRISTMAS DAY!!!

The Light of Christ

DONALD FISHEL

2. *God gave up His only Son*
   our of love for the world,
   so that all men who believe in Him
   will live forever.

3. *The light of God has come to us*
   so that we might have salvation;
   from the darkness of our sins we walk
   into glory with Christ Jesus.

Then the angel showed me the river of the water of life, as clear as crystal, flowing from the throne of God and of the Lamb down the middle of the great street of the city. On each side of the river stood the tree of life, bearing twelve crops of fruit, yielding its fruit every month. And the leaves of the tree are for the healing of the nations. No longer will there be any curse. The throne of God and of the Lamb will be in the city, and his servants will serve him. They will see his face, and his name will be on their foreheads. There will be no more night. They will not need the light of a lamp or the light of the sun, for the Lord God will give them light. And they will reign for ever and ever.

The angel said to me: "These words are trustworthy and true. The Lord, the God of the spirits of the prophets, sent his angel to show his servants the things that must soon take place."

"Behold, I am coming soon! Blessed is he who keeps the words of the prophecy in this book."

I, John, am the one who heard and saw these things. And when I had heard and seen them, I fell down to worship at the feet of the angel who had been showing them to me. But he said to me, "Do not do it! I am a fellow servant with you and with your brothers the prophets and of all who keep the words of this book. Worship God!"

Then he told me. "Do not seal up the words of the prophecy of this book, because the time is near. Let him who does wrong continue to do wrong; let him who is vile continue to be vile; let him who does right continue to do right; and let him who is holy continue to be holy."

"Behold, I am coming soon! My reward is with me, and I will give to everyone according to what he has done. I am the Alpha and the Omega, the First and the Last, the Beginning and the End.

"Blessed are those who wash their robes, that they may have the right to the tree of life and may go through the gates into the city.   *Revelation 22: 1–14*

The Day After...

IF STORE CLERKS THOUGHT they were over-worked during the Christmas shopping season, what must it be like the day after. People bring in gifts to exchange sizes, colors, and even styles. Then there are those who received cash gifts and are in line to make thrifty buys during the sales. But unless there is a real discount, one counter will not be busy–the display of Christmas decorations. The reason? Christmas is over, or for some people it is.

In most of the world, we Christians have just celebrated the birth of Jesus who came so that everybody might have a more abundant life. We have sung and read about Him and we have known the joy of loving and giving to others. Are we now to lay it all aside like we do the Christmas decorations? Are we to invite the non-Christians to wonder "Where is He who only yesterday was reborn as King of these people?" Show them that He lives in your heart.

God gave us our Savior as a gift of love, and we who have received this gift must not fall into the trap of loving as the world loves. Dare to be different. It is easy to love the people who love and accept us and those who have been good to us. It may be difficult, but not impossible, to love those who have mistreated us and do not deserve it.

Do not let Christmas be over. It is a story of love and we need to pass it on every day. Allow God to love from within you and you will find His extension will allow you to love those who need it most–those who have nothing to give and those who have stumbled in a world of darkness.

Prayer: Help us, Heavenly Father, to express your love every day and to keep your Spirit of Christmas alive in our hearts. Amen.

Applying Our Gift: "Jesus loves me, this I know, for the Bible tells me so."   Hymn by Anna B. Warner

Proclaim Joy

You who bring good tidings to Zion,
 go up on a high mountain.
You who bring good tidings to Jerusalem,
 lift up your voice with a shout,
lift it up, do not be afraid;
 say to the towns of Judah,
 "Here is your God!"
See, the Sovereign Lord comes with
 power,
 and his arm rules for him.
See, his reward is with him,
 and his recompense accompanies him.
He tends his flock like a shepherd:
 He carries the lambs in his arms
and carries them close to his heart;
 he gently leads those that have young.
     Isaiah 40: 9–11

VERSES IN TODAY'S SCRIPTURE makes one mindful of the American folk song that we sing at Christmas.

"Go, tell it on the mountains,
 Over the hills and everywhere;
 Go, tell it on the mountains
 That Jesus Christ is born!"

We can sense the joy proclaimed in both the Scripture and the song. Isaiah says "Lift up your voice with a shout, lift it up, do not be afraid." The song tells us to spread the Good News of Jesus Christ everywhere!

Although the shepherds feared and trembled during the angels' visit, they got up, went to Bethlehem, found the Child and worshipped. Luke 2:17 tells us that "they spread the word concerning what had been told them about this child." They were the first people to share the great joy of Jesus' birth.

I like to believe that these shepherds were familiar with the Isaiah passage, particularly verse eleven where Jesus is described as a shepherd. These tender, loving words would have held great meaning for them as they cared every day for their flocks, carrying the lambs and gently leading their sheep.

Jesus proclaimed Himself to be our good shepherd (John 10:11ff). He promised to lead and protect us. He said He would lay down His life for His sheep. This He did on the cross of Calvary, bringing us salvation and victory over sin and death.

What Joy we find here. Jesus' work of salvation is complete, but still He continues to be our Shepherd–providing rest, peace, and joy. May we do our part as the shepherds did–spreading the good tidings with boldness and love.

Prayer: Dear Heavenly Father, one of the gifts that we receive through Your Spirit is JOY–the joy of salvation and of the Lordship of Jesus Christ. Help us to claim this gift and freely give it to others. In Jesus' Name. Amen.

Applying the Gift: This news is too good to keep to ourselves!

How Will They Know

Then he said to his disciples, "The harvest is plentiful, but the workers are few. Ask the Lord of the harvest, therefore, to send out workers into his harvest field."

Matthew 9: 37, 38

We've a story to tell to the nations
That shall turn their hearts to the
** right,**
A story of truth and mercy,
A story of peace and light,
A story of peace and light. *

**Hymn "We've a Story to Tell*
to the Nations"
Text and Music: H. Ernest
Nichol

ELABORATELY DECORATED HIGH RISE department stores glitter in bright reds, greens, and golds, and "O Come All Ye Faithful" plays as I make my way through the crowds inside. Downtown New York City during the Christmas shopping rush? No, I was in Tokyo, Japan. Upon seeing these sights and hearing the old familiar Christian Christmas tunes in my own language, I found joy at the time of year when I long the most to be at home with family and friends enjoying our American Christmas traditions. Quickly my joy faded as I realized that the message of Christmas is barely known in this land of over 120 million where less than one percent claim to be Christian.

The most cherished Japanese holiday is New Years when annually thousands trek to Buddhist and Shinto shrines to offer coins and prayers to various impersonal gods for good fortune in the coming year. As in America, it seems the Christmas season is an answer to these prayers, as commercialism brings great profits to many merchants.

Some Christmas customs have carried over to Japan. They have a big Christmas day dinner, exchange gifts, and spend time with family and friends. As I see these customs transferred, I gain hope that one day the true meaning of Christmas will be a part of every day here in Japan—that Jesus Christ was born this day, in the East, to bring the gift of salvation to men of all nations.

Prayer: Father God, I ask for more Christians to come to Japan to tell about You. I ask that You would help us remember to pray for those called to serve as missionaries around the world. Open our eyes and ears to Your calling and direction. Amen.

Applying the Gift: We must show the power of the resurrected Lord to the unsaved millions in the world so that they may know of His salvation. God could easily save them without us, but He has chosen to use us as His instruments. Will we heed His call to live holy lives, to pray, and to let the Holy Spirit's power overflow into the lives of the unsaved around us?

I'm Coming

I'm coming, the day will be here soon
Come out, stay pure, oh child keep true
Though deception fill the land
Know my promise is at hand
My word is true. I will not fail you.

Look for Me, I tell you it won't be long
Cling to Me and by My strength stay strong
Watch and wait my friend
See the working of My plan
My word is true. I will not fail you.

Chorus:
This is the word of the Lord my friend
He who endures until the end
Will be crowned with a crown made of precious gems
And dwell in the House of the Lord.
Keep your eyes on Him. Just keep your eyes
on Him, Keep your eyes on Him.

Abide in Me, live your life in My light.
Dwell in My word let it be your delight.
Don't grow weary in what you do
Know your Shepherd's coming soon
and My word is true, I will not fail you.

(Repeat Chorus)

Peggy Carlson

Christmas world round

"…and you will be my witnesses
in Jerusalem, and in all Judea
and Samaria, and to the
ends of the earth."
      —Acts 1:8b

This is how the birth of Jesus Christ came about: His mother Mary was pledged to be married to Joseph, but before they came together, she was found to be with child through the Holy Spirit. Because Joseph her husband was a righteous man and did not want to expose her to public disgrace, he had in mind to divorce her quietly.

But after he had considered this, an angel of the Lord appeared to him in a dream and said, "Joseph son of David, do not be afraid to take Mary home as your wife, because what is conceived in her is from the Holy Spirit. She will give birth to a son, and you are to give him the name Jesus, because he will save his people from their sins."

All this took place to fulfill what the Lord had said through the prophet: "The virgin will be with child and will give birth to a son, and they will call him Immanuel"—which means, "God with us."

When Joseph woke up, he did what the angel of the Lord had commanded him and took Mary home as his wife. But he had no union with her until she gave birth to a son. And he gave him the name Jesus.

Matthew 1: 18–25

The thief comes only to steal and kill and destroy; I have come that they may have life, and have it to the full.

John 10:10

Christmas In Colombia

In Colombia at Christmastime nearly every home has a pesebre, which is a model of a manger scene plus all of Bethlehem and the surrounding countryside. The figures and buildings are saved from year to year and added to, but the setting is created new each Christmas, resulting in a different and usually more elaborate scene each time. The entire Christmas story is depicted, including the village with its homes and the inn that had no room, plus the shepherds with their sheep outside the town and the visit from the angels. The more enthusiastic pesebre builders will fill an entire room with their creation.

Sometimes the pesebre will include items from modern Colombian life that most certainly were not a part of the original setting. People identify so closely with the birth of Christ that they do not draw a line between the time of Christ and now. They have grasped the truth that the birth of Christ is for us today as well as for the people of the first century A.D. Jesus came to save us who live in the 1900's from our sins and to give us abundant life. He came wanting to be a part of our lives and lovingly wanting to do for us the things we cannot do for ourselves. He came to bridge the gap between us sinful human beings and the holy and perfect God.

Prayer: Jesus, we thank you for coming to earth to die for our sins and make it possible for us to know God. Thank You, too, for the abundant life we can have in You. Help us to live it. Amen.

Applying Our Gift: Let us celebrate this Christmas by humbly surrendering our lives to Jesus Christ and allowing Him to do for us all the things we cannot do for ourselves.

Standing Forever

"Comfort, comfort my people, says your God. Speak tenderly to Jerusalem, and proclaim to her that her hard service has been completed, that her sin has been paid for, that she has received from the Lord's hand double for all her sins.

A voice of one calling: "In the desert prepare the way for the Lord; make straight in the wilderness a highway for our God. Every valley shall be raised up, every mountain and hill made low; the rough ground shall become level, the rugged places a plain. And the glory of the Lord will be revealed, and all mankind together will see it. For the mouth of the Lord has spoken."

A voice says, "Cry out." And I said, "What shall I cry?"

"All men are like grass, and all their glory is like the flowers of the field. The grass withers and the flowers fall, because the breath of the Lord blows on them. Surely the people are grass. The grass withers and the flowers fall, but the word of our God stands forever."

Isaiah 40: 1–8

A FEW YEARS AGO, a ball point pen company introduced a pen with erasable ink to the market. The product came with an eraser attached to the other end—much like a pencil. Businesses and agencies replied negatively to the new product because they rely on signed contracts and documents. Banks, for example, were concerned about the ease with which checks could be altered. Government bureaus were similarly ruffled about changing various paper forms. Our society depends a great deal on the written word to keep records, and the new pen threatened the permanence of written words.

How different is the Word of our God. It stands forever! In Isaiah's prophecy this "Word" is a declaration from God. During Advent we look forward to the coming of the Word made flesh. Both the prophecy and the flesh are words from God, and each stands forever, not because of paper and ink, nor even chisel and stone, but because they are from God. Christians, we have an everlasting foundation for life!

Prayer: Holy God, even Your Word stands forever! May we be given the grace to trust You and live eternally. Amen.

Applying the Gift: Sound may fall on the ear, but God's Word stands forever.

OFFERING OUR WORSHIP

Epiphany

As a top
Invisible by height
Of energy
Gathers random light
In a transparency of Christmas colors
Occasional oblation,
Not always costly as our talents,
Are burnished to incandescence
Spinning since a certain night.

All three kings knelt,
Not only to another king
But lower,
That their gifts
Be known to One newborn
In darkness of the cave;
Innocent that offerings,
Energy of praise,
Intended for the Child,
Are luminous
With His delight.

Eleanore Nevin

Twelfth Night or Epiphany is the traditional name given to the holy day celebrated in some Christian churches on January 6. Since the 300's the day has honored the meeting of the three wise men, called the Magi, with the infant Jesus.

Introduction to Worship

"Yet a time is coming and has now come when the true worshipers will worship the Father in spirit and truth, for they are the kind of worshipers the Father seeks. God is spirit, and his worshipers must worship in spirit and in truth." John 4: 23, 24

THERE IS NO GREATER GOAL in life than to worship God in Spirit and in Truth. It may be said that the Bible is a book about worship–the worship of God. Worship is the unique act of acknowledging who God is, what he has done, and recognizing our relationship to Him. It may help to remember that our English word "worship" comes from the same root as does worth. To worship is to "worth-ship" Him, seeing Him as being of greatest value. Scripture is brimming with this theme.

"And I saw a mighty angel proclaiming in a loud voice, 'Who is worthy to break the seals and open the scroll?'…And they sang a new song:

'You are worthy to take the scroll
and to open its seals,
because you were slain,
and with your blood you
purchased men for God
from every tribe and language and
people and nation.
You have made them to be a kingdom to
serve our God
and they will reign on the earth.'

"Then I looked and heard the voice of many angels, numbering thousands upon thousands, and ten thousand times ten thousand. They encircled the throne and the living creatures and the elders. In a loud voice they sang:

'Worthy is the Lamb, who was slain,
to receive power and wealth and
wisdom and strength
and honor and glory and praise!'

"Then I heard every creature in heaven and on earth and under the earth and on the sea, and all that is in them singing:

'To him who sits on the throne and
to the Lamb
be praise and honor and glory
and power,
for ever and ever!'" Revelation 5: 2, 9–13

God in His beauty allows many possibilities of approach to worship.

We Have Come To Worship Him

After Jesus was born in Bethlehem in Judea, during the time of King Herod, Magi from the east came to Jerusalem and asked, "Where is the one who has been born king of the Jews? We saw his star in the east and have come to worship him."

Matthew 2: 1–2

After they had heard the king, they went on their way, and the star they had seen in the east went ahead of them until it stopped over the place where the child was. When they saw the star, they were overjoyed. On coming to the house, they saw the child with his mother Mary, and they bowed down and worshiped him. Then they opened their treasures and presented him with gifts of gold and of incense and of myrrh. And having been warned in a dream not to go back to Herod, they returned to their country by another route.

Matthew 2: 9–12

MANY HAVE SPECULATED as to the identity of the "Magi" from the East. Some say they were astrologers, some report that they were kings or leaders in foreign lands, and some say they were simply nomads that had a vision; but it does not matter how great they were, only that they knew that the bright star in the East would lead them to the King of the Jews whom they wished to worship.

At this time of year, people gather at many churches to worship Jesus and remember how the wise men were guided to Bethlehem nearly two thousand years ago. May our hearts be full of joy as we remember over three hundred promises of a coming Messiah, expressed by many different voices at many different times. Jesus, our Savior fulfilled them all.

May our hearts be prepared to worship our eternal God who, on the holy night that we celebrate, took on human flesh and lived on earth as a man. He did not just become man; He became God-man, genuine humanity without sin! He loves us; let us love Him, too!

Like the Wise Men, let us worship Him.

Prayer: Dear God, thank You for Christmas. Give us the wisdom of the Magi to follow Your star and to take the road on which You lead us. Amen.

Applying the Gift: Wise men still seek him.

A Prayer For The New Year

Almost everyone knows the Lord's prayer. In old war movies G.I.'s would repeat it while bombs exploded around them. In new TV shows either priests or nuns can be heard saying at least portions of it. As a very young child, I learned it from non-Christian parents who believed it was important for me to memorize. Down through the years I said it along with another little prayer, and felt safe and secure at night when the room was dark and I was all alone.

After experiencing the new birth, the prayer took on new meaning for me because when I said, "Our Father," I understood He was truly my Father. But it was not until this morning that I saw the Lord's Prayer in a new and wonderful light. The Lord's Prayer is my Father's New Year's gift.

Do not be like them, for your Father knows what you need before you ask him.

"This, then, is how you should pray:

" 'Our Father in heaven,
hallowed be your name,
your kingdom come.
your will be done
on earth as it is in heaven.
Give us today our daily bread.
Forgive us our debts,
as we also have forgiven our debtors.
And lead us not into temptation,
but deliver us from the evil one.' "

Matthew 6: 8–13

RELATIONSHIP (OUR FATHER)—As His children we can approach Him as Abba or Daddy, and expect to receive all that a good, loving father would give: food, shelter, direction, encouragement, discipline, instruction, compassion, forgiveness, understanding, tenderness—in short, love.

WORSHIP (HALLOWED BE THY NAME)—As His creation we should remember He alone is worthy of our praise, adoration and honor. Only He should receive our bended knee, our confessions, our total obeisance. We should be willing to present our bodies on the altar as a living sacrifice and allow Him to enliven us spiritually and use us in acceptable service.

KINGSHIP (THY KINGDOM COME, THY WILL BE DONE)—As His subjects, we should also approach Him as the King He is, giving Him total allegiance, fidelity and loyalty. As His servants we should submit to Him in every area, and respond with proper awe to His sovereignty.

DEPENDENCE (GIVE US…DAILY)—We recognize our total dependence on Him. He provides us with our daily needs, both physical and spiritual, and as our Father, lovingly withholds that which He determines would be detrimental.

FAILURE (FORGIVE US)—We recognize our failure. We need Him not only to give but to forgive—forgiveness initially, to bring us into His relationship, but also daily, to maintain our fellowship with Him. Because of this forgiveness, He expects us to willingly forgive others.

TRIUMPH (DELIVER US)—And we recognize His triumph over sin and Satan. Knowing He has delivered us from the bondage of sin, we yield to Him daily, experiencing deliverance from the temptations of sin.

For me, New Year's resolutions are "for the birds." But a New Year's revelation, that is something else. Have a blessed and prayerful new year.

FOR THINE IS THE KINGDOM AND THE POWER AND THE GLORY FOREVER. AMEN.

Be A Walking Temple

Therefore, I urge you, brothers, in view of God's mercy, to offer your bodies as living sacrifices, holy and pleasing to God—this is your spiritual act of worship. Do not conform any longer to the pattern of this world, but be transformed by the renewing of your mind. Then you will be able to test and approve what God's will is—his good, pleasing and perfect will.

Romans 12: 1, 2

OFFERING OUR BODIES as living sacrifices, holy and pleasing to God, is a most powerful witness to those around us. Testimony through action, perhaps even void of words, is Christ's influence on display. You have probably heard the sayings, "talk is cheap," "actions speak louder than words," "do as I say not as I do." Living Christianity as a holy, "set apart" person provides the powerful example in action, not only a definition in words.

Christians are "set apart," holy, and can be distinguished from those who do not believe. One way to be set apart is for us as Christians to isolate or separate ourselves from the rest of the world and be involved only in activities and only with people who share our bond in Christ. Certainly this would make us holy and set apart; however, it may also mean being hidden. Being hidden keeps our testimony from influencing nonbelievers.

The challenge comes in being set apart and not being separated—being distinguishable from the crowd while still being in the crowd. Living a lifestyle consistent with the Bible in our society means non-conformity and sometimes sacrificing what this world views as pleasurable or important. This involves forsaking conformity, standing out in a crowd, and allowing God's Spirit to transform us by renewing our minds. Renewing our minds means thinking differently, talking differently, and particularly, acting differently. This different activity is worship, in the temples of the Holy Spirit, our lives.

Think about the possibility of a walking temple which is God's house, where He and His Spirit reside: the place where God's people gather to worship Him; in Old Testament days, a place to offer sacrifices, a holy place set apart; a house which is distinct from other houses.

Prayer: Lord, transform me by Your Spirit into Your image that others may know of my faith. Help me strive to continuously improve my witness in action and word in order to further glorify You. Give me discernment in my behaviors and lifestyle to choose those who glorify You over those who hamper my testimony. Thank You for Your patience in my transformation and understanding in my blemishes. May You be glorified through the fruits of my witness. Amen.

Applying Our Worship: Today, consciously remember that you are a walking temple of God and His Spirit. List the changes you make because of this.

Sacrifices

Words by Bryan Jeffery Leech
Music by Bryan Jeffery Leech and Steve Wilkinson

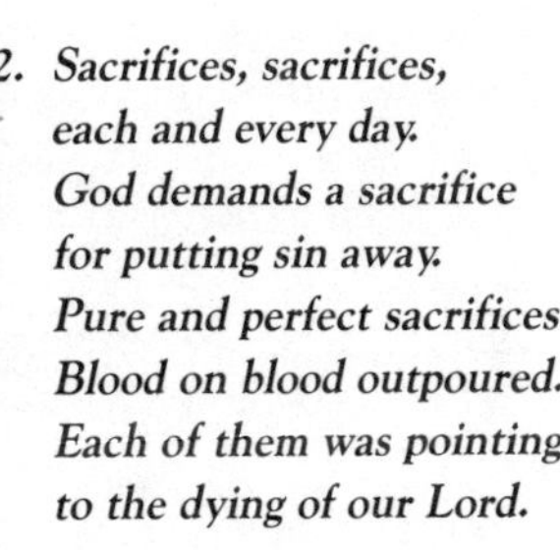

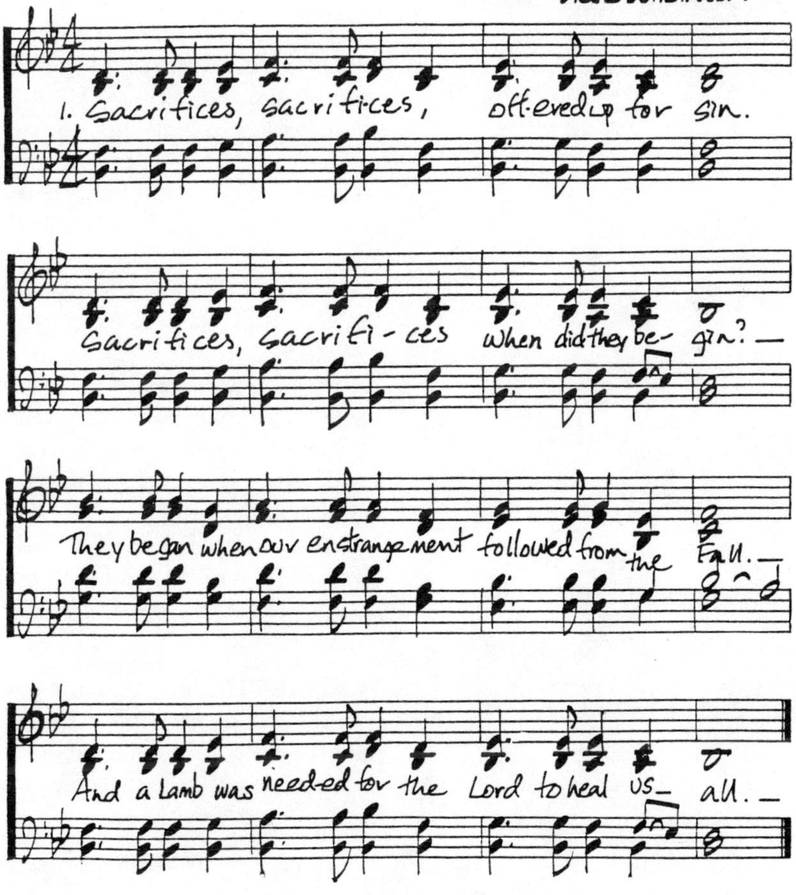

2. *Sacrifices, sacrifices,*
each and every day.
God demands a sacrifice
for putting sin away.
Pure and perfect sacrifices
Blood on blood outpoured.
Each of them was pointing
to the dying of our Lord.

3. *Sacrifices, sacrifices,*
then one offering more.
Christ became the Paschal Lamb
To show what lambs are for.
Out of love our gifts we give Him
In a thousand ways.
Everything becomes to Him
a sacrifice of praise.

4. *Sacrifices, sacrifices,*
deeds and praise and prayer.
Love poured out before the Lord
Like incense in the air.
In our hearts and in our words.
We give you Lord your due.
Every day in every way
We give ourselves to you.

Who Was The Witness?

WHILE WATCHING THE FILM of a parade on television we noticed some bystanders holding up signs. My son remarked that he was reminded of a fan in the stands at a football game who held up a sign reading John 3:16. He had been inspired to look up the reference in his Bible and asked, "What does that have to do with the game?"

My first reply was to quote the reference verbatim which, on second thought, was intended more to impress than to inform. Then I suggested (from previous experience with non-believers) that perhaps they were being facetious, intending to ridicule. At this point the conversation was redirected to another subject.

Later, having difficulty sleeping, I began to reflect upon our conversation, realizing I had muffed an opportunity to explain the good news. The Holy Spirit revealed to me that indeed it has everything to do with the game–the most important "game of life." Without "believing in Him," the game is lost.

It is true that we (mankind) are basically sinful; we are envious, greedy, lustful and dishonest, and fall short of God's image for which He designed us. To restore that image (to be like Him and become a member of His family) He sent His Son, Jesus, to die on a cross taking upon Himself our deserved punishment. All that is left for us is to believe and confess this sacrifice of Jesus Christ for ourselves and we are thereby justified (just-as-if-I had never sinned) before God, becoming a member of His family to live with Him forever–Eternal Life.

Who was the witness in this story? Was it the football fan in the stands? Was it God's Word, the Bible? Was it the Holy Spirit speaking to my conscience? Or, will it be this devotion which provides the opportunity to recover what I earlier muffed?

Prayer: Dear Father, You love me so much that You give me repeated opportunities to come into the right relationship with You. First is that all-important decision to ask You to be Savior of my life, and Lord, I ask that now. Help me to tell others the good news. Help me be ready to speak for You. In Jesus' Name. Amen.

Applying Our Worship: The good news is the gift to be accepted and shared.

Start Listening!

As Jesus walked beside the Sea of Galilee, he saw Simon and his brother Andrew casting a net into the lake, for they were fishermen. "Come, follow me," Jesus said, "and I will make you fishers of men." At once they left their nets and followed him.

When he had gone a little farther, he saw James son of Zebedee and his brother John in a boat, preparing their nets. Without delay he called them, and they left their father Zebedee in the boat with the hired men and followed him.

Mark 1: 16–20

ON A VISIT TO CHICAGO, I rode the train to a friend's house. Having grown up in a rural area, riding public transportation is always an adventure.

When I got on the train, my ears strained to hear the stops announced. I was very anxious that I would not miss my stop. While I strained my ears to listen, across the aisle a young woman slept! It was beyond my comprehension how she could sleep. I was so nervous I could barely sit! Then I remembered back to my earlier church days when I learned to sleep through the "long prayer" and wake up when I heard AMEN. I ventured to guess that her mind only heard her stop.

I thought a little more and reflected on my own spiritual journey through life. Much of the time, I fear that I lull myself to sleep. I train my mind to listen only for the things I want to hear. I can conveniently "sleep" through the challenges and charges God is calling out. I hear fellowship and I am ready; I hear prayer and I am tired. I hear retreat and I am eager; I hear Bible study and I am asleep. I hear potluck and I am there; I hear committee meeting and I am in a coma!

How much God longs for us to hear all He has to say instead of listening so selectively. We need to sit anxiously on the edge of our "pews" straining to hear God call our name. We do this not out of fear that we will be lost if we do not. We listen keenly because we know that when He calls for us to grow and to serve, life will be filled with excitement, joy, and a sense of fulfillment.

Prayer: Dear Lord, we want to hear You, but our own selves seem to get in the way. Help us listen actively to You–and respond. In Jesus' Name. Amen.

Applying Our Worship: Do not go to sleep! Do not selectively listen. You may block out the opportunity of a lifetime. God is going to call you. Are you going to be listening?

Standing On The Promises Of Christ My King

WHEN I THINK OF "standing on the promises" I think of the joy and peace I have because of my belief. My belief in Jesus is threefold: believing, trusting, and relying.

Believe in Jesus and be saved. This is what the Bible says. Believing takes an extra measure of faith because we have to have faith in the unseen. Only by the Spirit of God does this occur. This is the first and most important part of belief.

Trusting takes time and energy. It takes time to allow ourselves to trust God that He will take care of things no matter what, and energy to trust God, to allow Him to do His will in our lives.

Relying is the most vital part of belief. I think it is relatively easy to believe in Jesus and to give our lives to Him when we see who and what He is. He created the world out of nothing! But relying on the Lord takes work–much work. Relying means relaxing in the Lord, knowing that if we give Him our lives that He is going to use it in the best possible way.

What peace–inner peace–we will have if we can learn with the help of the Spirit to believe, trust and rely on the Lord.

> Standing on the promises that cannot fail,
> When the howling storms of doubt and fear assail,
> By the living Word of God I shall prevail,
> Standing on the promises of God. *

Prayer: Dear Lord, Your promises will not fail! Help me to stand on this truth. Amen.

Applying Our Worship: Where are peace and joy lacking in your life? Are you believing, trusting, and relying on the Lord in these situations?

Giving God Our Undivided Attention

THIS OLD TESTAMENT SCRIPTURE, begins

> "Hear, O Israel: The Lord our God, the Lord is one. Love the Lord your God with all your heart and with all your soul and with all your strength..."

The Lord is speaking about commitment. He covets our complete devotion to Him. However, the major and minor distractions which we allow into our daily lives are vast hindrances to commitment.

How often does our Father have our undivided attention? As human beings, the attention we give to God is generally divided attention. Our minds wander during prayer time, worship, and Bible reading. In fact, some days we forget about Him altogether. We are weak creatures, unable to give God our total commitment.

However, God pours our His blessings onto His weak children by saying

> "My grace is sufficient for you, for my power is made perfect in weakness."

Paul adds his comment to God's promise in II Corinthians 12:9:

> "Therefore, I will boast all the more gladly about my weaknesses, so that Christ's power may rest on me."

How can we, with our weak, divided attention be effective for the kingdom of God? Through grace. His grace is sufficient; we have His assurance. Grace overcomes divided attitudes. As God gains our undivided attention, our faith begins to grow. As faith grows, our ineffective lives become strong and powerful and have the ability to minister with compassion and love to the people whose lives we touch.

Prayer: Faithful God quiet our hearts and minds and cause our divided attention to become undivided toward You. Fill us with the power of Your Holy Spirit to work effectively for Your kingdom. Amen.

Applying Our Worship: Be at peace, knowing that God promises to turn the weak and divided Christian into an undivided and powerful minister of love.

Devotion
or
Am I A Pacifist?

EVEN THOUGH I BELIEVE IN GOD, I make no effort to let even my mate know it. Although we live side by side, I let every chance or opportunity pass to show how I feel about my Maker.

How devoted am I? Is Jesus in my mind? Do I tell about what He has done for me each day? Do I ever give praise to the Lord and thereby give credit to Him for each daybreak, for each sunset, for blue skies, for green trees, brown dirt, red roses, blue violets and white lilies? Do I speak of these things to others? And, if I do, do I say how great and magnificent our God is?

When I feel the warmth of a hug from a child or see its eyes twinkle, do I realize this baby is a gift from God—not just to its parents but to me and to the world?

Do I stop to think how miserable life must be to some who cannot enjoy the sound of children playing?

Do I plant ideas and dreams into the minds of children the Lord sends to me? Do I whisper prayers into babies' ears when their mom lets me hold them? Do I tell them Jesus loves them, and not just, "You are cute—you have pretty clothes—you are great?" Do I not give God the credit He deserves from the first? Early teaching about Jesus to ears that are listening is important.

Have I done all the things I wanted to do today before I spent time with You? Did I write love letters to my children and to my friends? Did I share my heart or cover my thoughts with empty words? How devoted am I?

Prayer: Lord, I am not where I want to be. Draw me to You. I ask for the Holy Spirit to replace the spirit of depression that is spreading in our country, churches, homes, families, and my life, with Your Spirit of joy, peace, patience, kindness, goodness, faithfulness, gentleness, self-control and love. Amen.

Applying Our Worship: Remember this: you, dear children, are from God and have overcome, because the One who is in you is greater than the one who is in the world.

The Pine Tree

"I am the true vine, and my Father is the gardener. He cuts off every branch in me that bears no fruit, while every branch that does bear fruit he prunes so that it will be even more fruitful. You are already clean because of the word I have spoken to you. Remain in me, and I will remain in you. No branch can bear fruit by itself; it must remain in the vine. Neither can you bear fruit unless you remain in me.

"I am the vine; you are the branches. If a man remains in me and I in him, he will bear much fruit; apart from me you can do nothing. If anyone does not remain in me, he is like a branch that is thrown away and withers; such branches are picked up, thrown into the fire and burned. If you remain in me and my words remain in you, ask whatever you wish, and it will be given you. This is to my Father's glory, that you bear much fruit, showing yourselves to be my disciples.

John 15: 1–8

WHEN I WAS IN THE MOUNTAINS RECENTLY, I was looking at a pine tree, a beautiful creation of God. As I studied the tree, I noticed how the lower limbs were dead and falling away, the branches in the middle were full and alive, and the branches on top were small.

In the same way, we grow in the Lord. Those lower limbs that do not glorify the Lord are taken away and destroyed because they are no longer necessary for growth. The branches in the middle compare with where we are now. However, these branches should be full and alive, as we are to be in Christ. The branches on top which are small and not yet fully formed are like the new areas of our lives where God is changing us, giving us new areas of growth.

Consider the root system of the pine tree. It has to be almost as big as the tree. The roots grow by taking minerals, water, and nutrients from the soil. The roots change the nutrients into food for life. This is what we must do by worshipping the Lord, reading the Bible, studying, praying, and fellowshipping with other Christians.

Prayer: Dear Lord, make me like a pine tree, growing toward You and being firmly rooted in You. Thank You for dying on the cross for me. Amen.

Applying Our Worship: Take a good look at a pine tree and at your life. Are you allowing the Lord to do His pruning?

Therefore, if anyone is in Christ, he is a new creation; the old has gone, the new has come!

II Corinthians 5: 17

Gifts for Charles

*You gave me back the rain
because we shared it,
and I learned that sharing
still could be.*

*You gave me back the music
because you made it,
and I learned anew
the glory of creativity.*

*You gave me back the laughter
because you caused it,
and as our minds played games,
I recalled my intellect.*

*You gave me back to honor
because you were gentle honesty,
and though I cannot understand,
your virtues are not suspect.*

*You gave me back to life
in all its gay variety,
and as we shared and sang and
    laughed,
I rejoined my humanity.*

*You gave me back to God,
because you lived him, too.
You gave so many lasting gifts;
My dear, what did I give you?*

Mavis Christensen

Extraordinary Reconciliation

CHRIST IS OUR RECONCILER. Adam and Eve's declaration of independence—disobedience—left God with two choices. God could either reciprocate the hostility or propose terms by which His rebellious subjects could return to peace. Not surprisingly, God sought to reestablish a loving relationship with his creations.

But God needed to address the problem of mankind's desire for independence from God. Insurrection had occurred and needed to be dealt with. Mankind needed to be instructed about the importance and beauty of a dependent relationship with God. God demonstrated His incomprehensible love and patience in the manner by which he provided this instruction.

He did not choose to instruct by punishment. Mankind's life without God had been miserable enough. He did not choose to instruct by abstract philosophy or religious instruction. Mankind was already burdened by such teachings beyond the ability to respond. Incomprehensively, God chose to teach mankind the necessity of dependence by example. God modelled His emphasis on dependence by coming to earth as the vulnerable baby-savior.

By seeking to serve rather than be served, Christ carried out God's desire to allow mankind to become His willing and joyful servants. By remaining vulnerable, even to the point of humiliating death, He demonstrated that in God's economy, serving is the end in itself and not the means to some other honorable goal.

By becoming our servant, Christ made it possible for us to regain the divine calling of giving, loving, and serving God and our fellow man. Furthermore, He has entrusted us with the privilege and responsibility of continuing the ministry of this extraordinary method of reconciliation.

Prayer: Heavenly Father, please empower me through Your reconciling, serving Holy Spirit to be an example and model of Your extraordinary method of reconciliation to the people You bring into my life. Amen.

Applying Our Worship: Is there a relationship in my life that needs improving? Using Christ's example, what steps can I take to bring that reconciliation?

I can do everything through him who gives me strength.
Philippians 4:13

God Gives Courage

How many times in our lives are we presented with a situation that seems impossible and that fills us with fear? How often do we give up on a battle or a dream because it seems hopeless? It is at these times that we must claim the promise that God is always with us. We truly can have victory in all the trials and challenges God sets before us by using His power and strength.

The past few years have presented many of these trials in my life. Both of our children were born prematurely and required several weeks of hospitalization before we could bring them home. They both had periods when they would stop breathing momentarily. We had to learn to watch for this and know how to respond. We were thrilled when they were able to come home, and yet we felt a great deal of fear also. We feared that we would not know how to take care of their special needs. But, moment by moment, as we needed it, God filled us with knowledge, patience and confidence. He showed us that these were His special children and we were not alone in our challenge of raising them. They are now healthy, strong children.

Just as God helped us through our children's difficult first years, He also gave us victory in one of our hardest battles. My husband is a recovered alcoholic. I must admit that the battle with this disease seemed hopeless! But my husband took the step of entering a treatment center and dedicating his life to Christ, and God healed him of this disease. Fear could have robbed our family of the joy this sobriety has brought about. Instead, we give all the glory to God, for truly it was His strength and grace that brought about this miracle.

We are now faced with a new challenge. Both my husband and I feel the Lord calling us to rededicate our lives and serve Him in a special way. At this point we do not know many of the details of God's plan, but we can rest in our faith. Time and time again, God has shown us that He will fight our battles with us and He will give us the wisdom we need–if we ask and trust!

Are you facing a challenge in your life that you fear will be more than you can handle? Remember, God did not give us a spirit of fear, but commands us to be courageous. He says to us, "Have I not commanded you? Be strong and courageous. Do not be terrified; do not be discouraged, for the Lord your God will be with you wherever you go." (Joshua 1:9)

Prayer: Lord Jesus, we thank You for the many challenges You set before us as part of Your plan to make us more like You. Please give us the strength and courage we need to continue in our journey of faith. In Your name. Amen.

Applying Our Worship: Do not let yourself miss out on the joys and rewards with which God will bless you during these "stretching" times. Be strong and courageous. God is with you!

"At times, God puts out a fresh and specific call to his children, a call to renewed vision, fresh commitment, and a willingness to follow Him to new and unfamiliar depths of faith. For me, it seems that now is such a time–a time for courage. Courage, to let the light of the Holy Spirit shine through us in a dark, hostile, and needy world. Courage, not to give up when our path becomes rough, and the light of truth we follow seems to grow dim. Courage, that only comes from understanding the power, the faithfulness, the love of our Lord Jesus Christ. **

* *by Jamie Owens-Collins from her album "A Time For Courage," Live Oak Records.*

Hearts Courageous

Words and Music by Jamie Owens-Collins and Dan Collins

2. *And when sorrow dims the light along our way,*
  help us to see each time of darkness thro' eyes of faith.
  A time for hope, a time for courage, knowing you will lead us through.
  And we'll march with hearts courageous after you.

Psalms of Cedar Knoll
IV

*The deer came quietly
in the night.
They stepped out
from between
the trees
called evergreen,*

*And walked
the silvered path
across the lawn,
and paused to taste
the river mist,
a presage to the dawn.*

*All three,
like statues
cast in fume,
raised their heads
and gazed
upon the moon.*

*And then,
silently
as they had come,
wraithlike,
dissolved
into the night.*

*And I,
who had not breathed,
felt peace descend
and take my hand,
and felt triply blessed
at these visions
heaven sends.*

*They seem to come
when I have need,
and they bring
gentleness
and a tiny glimpse
of the world
we all seek.*

*And when
I have enough,
a vast, unrolling screen
of beauty,
the door will open,
and I pass through
to a place of harmony,*

*Where the humble
and the meek
stand tall and unafraid,
where kind is might,
and the deer
do not come
solely in the night.*

Mavis Christensen

How The Lord Works In Our Lives

By way of background, I was born and raised in the mid-west. My mother was a devout Catholic, and my father by contrast, only set foot in church twice in his life that I can remember. For a non-church goer, however, he had a remarkable way of privately patterning his life and actions around a life that must have found favor with God.

God has sometimes strange and powerful ways of getting His message across to each of us. In the early 50's I married a girl from my home town. A year later she died a slow and painful death from a chronic kidney disease. At the time, that event was very difficult for me to understand. Why should she have suffered so, and why should I also have to suffer? That was also the time when God's message to man was brought home to me. I was given a book entitled the *Imitation of Christ* by Thomas à Kempis. This spiritual classic provided great strength and consolation then, and continues to do so now. It introduced me to meditative prayer and a one-on-one relationship with God which has been a part of my life since that time.

Within a short time I met Ellie. That marriage, which is now in our thirty-second year, and our four children are indeed a direct gift of God to me and one which I greatly cherish. While no marriage is perfect in all respects, looking back at our years together is a happy and a beautiful experience and one which I am extremely grateful to be a parter in.

In the early 60's I was diagnosed as having a fairly advanced stage of lymphonic cancer. A friend took me one day to a healing prayer service with the Claretian Fathers. Remember, this was in the early 1960's and "hands on" prayer over the sick was somewhat unusual to find, and definitely unusual to experience. I do not attribute my healing from that disease to prayer any more than I would attribute it to the radiation treatments. What it did, however, was convince me that as in the previous tragedy in my life, prayer is an essential element of our existence on earth. In this latter case, I became aware of how the prayer of "two or more together" is manifested. Some years after that, I again witnessed the emotional and physical healing power of prayer through the charismatic movements in the Christian churches.

It seems to me that I have been given through these years and experiences the fundamental message of the need to love one another. God's plan for man as I understand it and believe, is to love one another as His children and to love Him with all our hearts, minds and bodies. It is my firm conviction that we in the human family all share equally in the love of our Creator. It is both our responsibility and our joy to serve "Our Father," and to have patience in understanding His divine will for each of us.

A Rose Bush In Your Garden

As a rose bush in your garden, Lord,
I'd see you on your knee
Giving special, tender loving care
For blooms you'd hope to see.

The gentle way you'd sprinkle
Living water on just right,
With the Holy gleam from your precious
Son providing ample light.

And though I'd prick you with my thorns
You'd stay not far away;
But continue on so patiently
To help me through the day.

When one of my flowers failed to bloom,
No grudges would you bear.
Instead you'd trim away my wilting ways
And help me flourish there.

When evil weeds surround my roots,
Their goal to choke and kill,
You'd say, "Have faith," and pluck them out
Delivering through thy will.

IF YOU WERE THE HEAD GARDENER, and each rose bush in your garden represented a human soul, how would your garden fare? Would you take time each day to water, prune, pull weeds, and plant new seeds when necessary? Would these rose bushes be a priority in your life? Praise God, they are to Him!

It is easy to get caught up in ourselves and our own lives, seeing only the things we need or desire. We often become blind to the needs, both physical and spiritual, of those around us. I am so thankful that God is not like that! For what happens to a forgotten plant that is not watered? Human souls can be compared to this. If God forgot about us as often as we forget about others, there would be many lives lost. God's Word tells us to "Be devoted to one another in brotherly love. Honor one another above yourselves." (Romans 12:10) God also tells us "Each of you should look not only to your own interests, but also to the interests of others." (Philippians 2:4)

How we care for each other is a reflection of God, for we are His representatives–His hired gardeners. It is our responsibility to do a good job in order to bring God the glory He so deserves.

Prayer: Lord, help me to be a "green thumb" gardener as You are, bringing life to all in my care. Thank You for Your perfect example in the care You give us. Above all, let my caring bring all glory and honor to you, O Lord, for You alone are worthy to be praised! Amen.

Applying Our Worship: Our God is so good! Let us share His goodness by loving and caring for those around us, creating a blossom filled garden fragrant with the love of our Lord Jesus Christ!

I'd grow and bloom with your special love,
Having fragrance of your pardon,
How blessed I'd be to have a home
Within the Master's garden.

Alanna Bell

The Craftsman

ABOUT A HUNDRED YEARS AGO, a craftsman put together a wonderful unit of kitchen cabinets in a home. They were all made of clear redwood and finished nicely. The craftsman had done a thorough job and the cabinets were ready for service.

However, the passing of time and neglect caused the house and cabinets to fall into a state of disrepair. The house was destroyed, but the cabinets were salvaged and used for storage in the backroom of a drugstore. There they were painted numerous times and fell into greater disrepair. The cupboard doors were removed and the drawers disappeared. The soft redwood had become greatly marred and many of the shelves were missing. What had once been a beautiful unit of kitchen cabinets had become worthless junk.

When the owner of the drugstore went out of business, the new renter cast the cabinets aside, delivering them into the reluctant care of a friend. For months the cabinets occupied an insignificant place in the friend's garage. Then one day the new owner of the cabinets took a closer look at them and realized they were all clear redwood. He saw some value in these old discarded cabinets and decided to rebuild and refinish them.

He stripped, sanded and repaired to remove the old paint, scratches and deep mars that existed in the old, soft redwood. Sections of the unit were broken down so that drawers and shelves could be made. Over two hundred hours of patient work went into the completion of the restoration process, and enough materials were left over to make a lovely redwood desk.

Many neighbors and friends watched as he transformed worthless junk into beautiful and useful furniture. That furniture now occupies a place of honor in his living room, the most refined and stately area in his home; and because he is a preacher, he spends many long hours studying at the desk. His books are displayed in the cabinet unit behind him.

While he had been working on the project, the Lord had been speaking to him. God enlightened him and showed him that those old cabinets were just like his life: scratched, marred, painted over, incomplete and seemingly of no use to anyone; but one day the Mastercraftsman took charge of him. That Craftsman did a slow and patient transformation of a life that just about everybody had abandoned. There are still some mars, and the cabinet is not perfect, but it truly has been born again.

Thank you, Jesus!

O Gentle Potter's hands
with beautiful end in view,
Do you know how it feels to be clay
molded and pressed and spinned
Conformed to the image of You?

Helpless, formless, of no worth
It aches and hurts and
  my heart cries
Till Master Potter ends His work
and I am mirrored in His eyes.

Prudie Steenholdt

I urge, then, first of all, that requests, prayers, intercession and thanksgiving be made for everyone—for kings and all those in authority, that we may live peaceful and quiet lives in all godliness and holiness. This is good, and pleases God our Saviour, who wants all men to be saved and to come to a knowledge of the truth. For there is one God and one mediator between God and men, the man Christ Jesus, who gave himself as a ransom for all men—the testimony given in its proper time. And for this purpose I was appointed a herald and an apostle—I am telling the truth, I am not lying—and a teacher of the true faith to the Gentiles.

I want men everywhere to lift up holy hands in prayer, without anger or disputing.

I Timothy 2: 1–8

A Guide For Prayer Partners

JESUS SAID, "Where two or three come together in my name, there am I with them." (Matthew 18:20)

A prayer partnership must be centered on the Lord. Therefore, it is a three-way partnership, the two of you and the Lord. Be certain that this focus is truly a mental commitment, even though you "know" it in your hearts.

BEGIN your partnership slowly, joining each other to share and pray once a week. Use the telephone in between as you have need or as the Spirit leads.

SHARE Scripture together.
• Read verses the Lord has called to your attention that day.
• Read portions together—a psalm, a chapter, or less if it is heavy with meaning.

LIST prayer requests and topics. Some things to include are your personal and family needs, church concerns, governments at all levels, missionaries, the worldwide kingdom of God, and those who need to know the Lord.

BEGIN your prayertime with praise. Sometimes use a hymn or praise chorus, lifting up your voices singing praise. Consider God's many attributes and praise Him for them.

REMEMBER that prayer is talking to God. There is no need for sophisticated words or fancy phrases. Talk to God in the plain language you use every day. Just tell Him what is on your heart. You and your partner will feel more at ease, and you will be speaking honestly to God.

AS you pray together, there are two forms that your prayer might follow. You may take turns, with each of you praying a few sentences or even a paragraph or two. Or you may pray "conversationally," with one praying only a phrase or a sentence before the other prays. You will probably use a combination of these two.

USE the prayer list that you have prepared, but be aware that the Holy Spirit will guide you to other topics also.

IF you have a time limitation, set a timer so you have a few minutes to conclude your prayer after the timer rings.

AS you pray together regularly, you will find your relationship with each other and the Lord becoming more meaningful. Be ready to encourage each other and rely on each other, challenging and stretching each other.

UNDERSTAND that as individuals you will grow in different areas and at different rates. You will continue to be individuals, but your growth will cause you to complement each other more and more. Accept each other and yourselves as you are. God does!

REALIZE that this partnership will take time, energy and commitment. Sometimes there will be difficult times as one of you is struggling with pain, heartache, or Christian growth. During these times, though, the need for a prayer partnership is the most critical. From them come the sweet rewards of a closer walk together with the Lord.

EXPECT and watch for answers to your prayers. Be generous with your thanksgiving and praise before as well as after you see the answers.

AS God leads you in your praying, pray "big" prayers. Remember, with God, nothing is impossible. (Luke 1:37)

EXPECT God to be with you as you meet for prayer. You will not be disappointed!

THE POWER OF PRAYER

The day was long, the burden I had borne
Seemed heavier than I could longer bear
And then it lifted—but I did not know
Someone had knelt in prayer;
Had taken me to God that very hour,
And asked the easing of the load,
* and He,*
In infinite compassion, had stooped down
And taken it from me.

We cannot tell how often as we pray
For some bewildered one, hurt and distressed
The answer comes, and many times those hearts
Find sudden peace and rest.
Some one had prayed, and Faith, a reaching hand,
Took hold of God, and brought Him
* down that day!*
So many, many hearts have need of prayer:
* Oh, let us pray!*

Author unknown

There is a time for everything, and a season for every activity under heaven:
a time to be born and a time to die,
a time to plant and a time to uproot,
a time to kill and a time to heal,
a time to tear down and a time to build,
a time to weep and a time to laugh,
a time to mourn and a time to dance,
a time to scatter stones and a time to gather them,
a time to embrace and a time to refrain,
a time to search and a time to give up,
a time to keep and a time to throw away,
a time to tear and a time to mend,
a time to be silent and a time to speak,
a time to love and a time to hate,
a time for war and a time for peace.

What does the worker gain from his toil? I have seen the burden God has laid on men. He has made everything beautiful in its time. He has also set eternity in the hearts of men; yet they cannot fathom what God has done from beginning to end. I know that there is nothing better for men than to be happy and do good while they live.

—Ecclesiastes 3.1–12

For Simple Things.

I ask thee, Lord, for simple things—
A humble, honest heart that sings,
And work to do that vision brings.

Someone to love and to love me,
A modest home, a book, a tree,
And deep, abiding faith in Thee.

I ask Thee, Lord, for simple things,
For simple things in life, have wings!

Elizabeth Beck Davidson

"May the spirit of Him whose love is eternal
Be within you to refresh you,
Above you to bless you,
Around you to protect you,
Beneath you to bear you up,
Before you to lead you on,
One God, Infinite and Eternal,"
World without end.

—Amen

Rev. James Allie Davidson
(His own special Benediction)

Contributors' Notes

The Lord said to Abraham—"I will surely bless you and make your descendants as numerous as the stars in the sky—and through your offspring all nations on earth will be blessed because you have obeyed me."   *Genesis 22: 17a, 18*

DAVID ALEXANDER lives with his wife Char and daughter Kate in Taiwan where they are missionaries for the Reformed Church. He grew up in Canoga Park, CA, where he attended the Platt Ranch and New Hope Churches. Dave is a graduate of Azusa Pacific University (B.A.), New Brunswick Theological Seminary (M.A.) and Rutgers University (M.A.).

TERESA ALLISON is a housewife and new mother of baby Phillip. Until his birth she had been employed as a surgical technician. Presently she is a pastor's wife in ministry at Christ Community Church, St. Albert, Alberta, Canada.

THE REV. STEVEN ALLISON was recently ordained in the Reformed Church after graduating from Fuller Theological Seminary in Pasadena. After completing his undergraduate work at a California university in the Sacramento area, he travelled to the East Coast and attended Gordon Conwell Seminary in Massachusetts. He served with YWAM—Youth with a Mission for a time. His wonderful voice and heart were shared generously while he was intern at New Hope Church. He provided us with the Spanish translation of the "Invitation." (We wish him and Terre God's blessing at their first church.)

SALLY ANGEL, a graduate of Denison University and member of Woodland Hills First Baptist Church, is a homemaker and mother. She teaches Sunday School and Child Evangelism as well as ladies' Bible studies. Sally is also on the Board of the Christian Women's Club.

THE REV. PHILIP ASSINK, Pastor of New Hope Church, is married and the father of two sons. He is a graduate of Seattle Pacific University (B.A.) and Western Theological Seminary (M.Div.). Pastor Phil also serves on the Board of Trustees of the International Society of Christian Endeavor ('73–'87) and as a Reformed Church representative on the Governing Board of the National Council of Churches of Christ in the USA ('84–'87). He grew up in the Yakima, WA area.

ALANNA SHARPE BELL is a homemaker, mother, artist and member of Camarillo Baptist Church. Along with writing for this book, it is she that captured the likenesses for the family memory devotions.

JONE BOSCH is a Ph.D. student in Old Testament at Fuller; a graduate of Western Theological Seminary (M.Div.); and Hope College (B.A.). In addition to being a Bible study leader and struggling writer, Jone is a member of Hope Reformed Church, Holland, MI and associate member of New Hope Community Church. Jone, of Dutch heritage, grew up in the Holland, MI area.

WILLIAM BROWN III is a graduate of Los Angeles Pierce College (A.A.) and Children's Ministries Assistant at New Hope Church. He believes, "A day given to the Lord is never wasted." Over Memorial Day weekend he went to Mexico with the "Faith on Fire" outreach.

PEGGY KYBER CARLSON, child and servant of the Lord Jesus, is a graduate of Cal State University, Northridge (CSUN), preschool teacher and chapel leader. At New Hope Church she is a member of the choir, soloist, and guitar and chorus leader. She and her husband, John, are on the Missions Committee.

IDA CASSON was born in Lafayette, Louisiana and moved to Texas as a young child. She attended Prairie View College. In addition to her duties as a wife and mother, Ida serves on the Board of the Christian Women's Club and leads Friendship Bible Coffees. Also, she is President of the Deaconess Board and President of the Missionary Committee at First Baptist Church of Woodland Hills.

MAVIS GAROUTTE CHRISTENSEN is an alumnus of Mankato State University, Mankato, MN, where she is currently studying for a Masters in Psychology of Religion. She owns and operates Cedar Knolls Bed and Breakfast on the former Pierce family farm near Good Thunder, MN. Mavis is a prairie person, former teacher now substituting, and a former newspaper writer and editor. She is a member of United Methodist Church, Beauford, Minn., a member of the So. Minnesota League of Poets, a widow and mother of four children, grandmother, shepherdess, and appreciator of God's infinite bounty of good things. Her heritage is French and German.

SUE GILLILAND CLARK, wife and mother, is a graduate of UCLA in Linguistics. Sue has been an encourager, advisor, listener, and language and text editor for this book. Her many interests range from the development of a Resource Center at New Hope Church, walking for fitness, and organization administration to catering and collecting cookbooks. She is also a Bethel Bible Series student.

DAVID COVEN is the Creative Director and owner of Design Graphics in Scottsdale, AZ, where he recently moved to be near his family. David, of French and English heritage, grew up in the Cleveland, Ohio area. He is a graduate of The California Institute of the Arts (B.S.A.). The cover of this book is his artistic rendition of a photo by Bob Wilkinson.

DR. DALE DAILY, a graduate of Western Michigan University (B.A.) and the University of Southern California (Ph.D.) recently retired from teaching history at Canoga Park High School. Dale has also taught adult Sunday School at New Hope Church for many years. Traveling, a mountain cabin, writing, gardening, and a special grandson fill up his days now.

LOIS DeJAGER DAILY, wife, mother and grandmother, who is of Dutch heritage from Grand Rapids, MI, is a graduate of CSUN. She also recently retired from teaching English. Lois did most of the original text editing for this book. Her willingness, encouragement, and expertise were contributing factors in getting this book to press. Now that she is retired, she has more time for sewing, reading, and taking fun courses at Pierce College.

ELIZABETH BECK DAVIDSON, a graduate of Denison University who also attended Andover Newton Seminary, is a native of Pittsburgh, PA. She is a mother, grandmother, former missionary and pastor's wife, speaker, traveler and hostess every Christmas season for a Hymn-sing for the four San Fernando Valley churches she and Dr. Davidson served as interim pastor and wife.

THE REV. DR. JAMES A. DAVIDSON (1908–1984), B.A., B.D., S.T.M., Ph.D., was born and raised in Texas. After his graduation from Andover Newton Seminary and marriage in 1933, he and Elizabeth served four churches in the American Baptist Convention in Pittsburgh and Warren, PA, Brockton, MA, and White Plains, N.Y. Retiring in 1971, they moved to California to be near their sons and begin a series of interim ministries.

THE REV. RAY DeVRIES (1932–1982), B.A., Min.D., grew up in the Chicago area. He was a graduate of Wheaton College and Western Theological Seminary. Before serving churches in Wyoming, MI and Canoga Park and Pomona, CA, he was on the radio program "Key to Life Hour" in Holland, MI. Ray was Vice President of Special Services at Lexicon Music/Light Records when he and Carl Seal wrote "Fill Me with Thy Grace." He was on the board of directors of many Christian organizations in the Los Angeles area at the time of his death. He is a missed friend, pastor, musician, father and husband. His smile and the twinkle in his eye are not forgotten.

LT. COL. USAF (Ret.) RAYMOND R. FISCHER is a graduate of the University of Rochester (B.A.). Bob served his country twenty-seven and one-half years with a specialty in air defense operations. "Born, bred, and infinitely proud to be an American," expresses his sentiments. Since 1984, this husband, father, and grandfather, has worked for Boeing Aerospace in International Marketing.

FRAN GRALOW, an American with German, English and Scandinavian roots, works as a Wycliffe literary consultant and trainer of writers in Indian languages in Colombia, South America. Having grown up in the Platt Ranch Church, Canoga Park, CA, she is now a member of Lake Avenue Congregational Church, Pasadena, CA.

GLENN GREGG, who is a combination of Scottish, Irish, German and Scandinavian, and a graduate of CSUN (B.A., M.A.), served as Minister of Music, New Hope Church ('82–'87). He is presently Associate Minister of Music at First Evangelical Presbyterian Church, Renton, WA. Running a big, black Doberman named Benson (or vice versa) is one of his pastimes when home in Canoga Park, CA.

CAROLINE STROEBEL GRIP is a graduate of Cal State, Chico and a graduate student at Cal State, Sacramento. Carrie is a Program Administrator, having worked for Boy Scouts of America and Campfire, Inc. She also lifeguards and teaches swimming to children.

MARK GRIP, a family counseling intern, is employed as a Psychiatric Social Worker at the Stanford Home for Children, Sacramento, CA. He is a graduate of Cal State, Fullerton (B.A., M.S.). He and Carrie enjoy living near the skiing at Tahoe.

HAROLD M. HAKKEN, of Dutch heritage, is a husband, father, grandfather, and graduate of Hope College. As a retired church executive, he now serves as President of the Board, Laubach Literacy Council of San Diego County, Inc., and as a Laubach tutor. He is also a board member of both the Community Resource Center and the Rotary Club of Encinitas, CA. He and Mary Ruth are members of the Village Church, Rancho Santa Fe, CA.

MARY RUTH HAKKEN, also of Dutch heritage, is a housewife and mother, and a graduate of Hope College. She is a retired high school English teacher serving on the Bible Study and Women's Council, Village Church. Mary Ruth is also a member of the American Assn. of University Women and a Laubach tutor.

TERENCE HANEY, husband, father, grandfather, is a graduate of St. Thomas College, St. Paul, MN, and a member of St. Bernardine's Catholic Church, Woodland Hills, CA. He is owner of the Terence Haney Co., a consulting group. His family and his hobbies of remodeling and refinishing occupy his spare time.

MARIE HO, who was born in Hong Kong, now lives in the San Fernando Valley with her family. She is a graduate of U.C. Irvine (B.S. in Computer Science) and is working on an M.B.A. at Cal State, Northridge. Marie is a member of the Evangelical Formosan Church which shares the New Hope facility where she serves as the Director of Children's Ministries and as a co-worker with the youth group. She translated the "Invitation" into Chinese for this book.

CHERI HOOVER HOCHENEDEL, housewife and mother of three, has completed five years of Bible Study Fellowship. Cheri is a wedding coordinator and enjoys working with youth at New Hope Church where she and her family are members. Her heritage–Child of God, Norwegian, Dutch and German.

TINA HUDSON, wife and mother, is Marketing Director, VSP Personnel, Phoenix, AZ. She is on the Board of the Moon Valley Christian Women's Club and a Friendship Bible Coffee Coordinator. Tina is a member and substitute Sunday School teacher at Paradise Valley Envagelical Free Church. She also speaks at Christian Women's Clubs, a part of Stonecroft Ministry.

NORIKO IDE is a graduate of Sophia University (B.A.), Tokyo, Japan. She is a member of the Musashino Evangelical Free Church. Noriko, a friend of Sue and Scott Tamaoka, is responsible for the beautiful translation of the "Invitation" into Japanese.

JON ILLG, husband and father, is Minister of Music at the Santa Rosa, CA, Christian Church. He is a contract record producer and owner of Masterpiece Music Co. Jon is a vocal soloist, guitarist, and enjoys downhill skiing. His mother is Janice Knapp.

JANICE BERKEY KNAPP is a mother and grandmother, and a graduate of the Minnesota School of Business. She works as Administrative Asst., VP West Coast Div., Firstours/Carlson Travel Group. Janice is a member of New Hope Church and serves on the Grounds Planning Committee. She is National Chairman, Education Group, Embroiderers' Guild of America. Her hobbies are teaching needlework, cooking, gardening and singing.

ROBERT KISSLING of Las Virgines Printing, is the printer of this book. He was born in Santa Monica, CA, is a husband and father of five children. His family attends Woodland Hills Neighborhood Church (Missionary Alliance). He is a graduate of University of Southern California majoring in Business. His printing experience began in Jr. High. He became owner of Las Virgines Printing one month after high school graduation.

LANA KOVNER, another Texan, holds a Bachelors in Art from CSUN. As a busy wife and mother, she finds time to lead and coordinate Friendship Bible Coffees and use her talents to produce such things as the line drawing of New Hope Church. Her hobbies are antiques and arts and crafts.

DAVID MANLY, teacher and preacher, is a graduate of SUNY Albany (B.A., M.A.) and Columbia (Ed.D.) in New York. He has been a professor of Education at State University College, Geneseo, NY. for twenty-seven years. Dr. Manly is a certified local pastor, United Methodist Churches at Canadice and Allens Hill, NY.

SCOTT MANLY (1966–1987), USAF Academy Class of '88, was a Life Scout, valedictorian of his high school class, National Merit Scholarship finalist and academic honors Aeronautical Engineering major at the Academy. He was serving at Philmont Boy Scout Ranch when struck and killed by lightning at age 21, August 2, 1987.

VICKI McNEESE, who was born in Wyoming, attended Central Wyoming College. She is the mother of four boys, a grandmother, and Mildred Sturgeon's niece. She works as an auditor.

LYNN MIYATA, owner of Linko's Typography, did the typesetting for this book. She is also a wife and mother, and a graduate of the University of Hawaii. Japanese-American born and raised in Hawaii, she brings the "Gift of Aloha" to this book.

GREGG MRAMOR, husband, and father of two sons, attended Pierce College and now works as a printer in the container industry. Gregg owns a painting and house repair business. His hobbies are camping and participating in sports such as co-coaching his younger son's soccer team. Gregg has completed the two-year Bethel leadership training.

GEOFFREY NUDELL, music copyist for this book, is a graduate of Grove School of Music in the composing and arranging program. He is a Senior at CSUN. In addition to having been choir accompanist at New Hope Church for seven years, Geoff is also a free lance and studio musician specializing in woodwinds. His heritage is Russian and Italian.

ANN O'NEAL OTT, housewife, mother and grandmother, is a graduate of Huntingdon College, Montgomery, AL, (B.A.) in Sociology and English. She is a former school teacher now working as an Education Aide for the Los Angeles Unified School District. Ann is a Bible student and member of New Hope Church. Living next door to the Stroebels, she provided a lot of quick editing help and advice for this book.

JAN WILKINSON OTT, housewife and mother of two young children, graduated from El Camino High School, Woodland Hills, CA. She works as an insurance consultant for a pediatric medical group. Jan is a choir member and soloist at New Hope Church.

LUCILLE PONTIOUS, widowed when her husband, the Rev. Elry Pontious, was accidentally struck by a car, serves on the Board of Evangelistic Missions, Inc., which they were instrumental in founding as an outreach in the West Indies. They served the Beauford, MN, Church in the 1940's, After his death, Rev. Pontious' Bible was found open to: *"The righteous perish, and no one ponders it in his heart; devout men are taken away, and no one understands that the righteous are taken away to be spared from evil. Those who walk uprightly enter into peace; they find rest as they lie in death."* Isaiah 57: 1–2

PETER ROBINSON, Attorney at Law, and Director of Christian Conciliation Service of Los Angeles, is a member and elder of New Hope Church. Pete and his wife, Vickie, are the exhausted parents of twin babies, Sarah and Rachel.

ELMER SCHAEFER, husband and father of USAF Academy Senior, Paul, and nurse, Sue, is a graduate of the University of Pittsburgh. His commitment to his home, family and country is reflected in this businessman's challenge to commitment in this book. He is a member of St. Bernardine's Catholic Church, Woodland Hills, CA.

MARIANNE LAUBEN SCHAEFER, a graduate of Indiana State University, PA, is teaching third grade in a San Fernando Valley Christian school. The Child Evangelism ministry has been an avenue, along with teaching, for her to express Christ's love and concern for children. Marianne's holidays and vacations are times of happy reunions with family and friends.

JEAN SLAGTER, originally from Grand Rapids, MI, now mother, grandmother, and housewife, says she belongs to the "born to shop" Club (along with some of the rest of us), and her husband, John was "born to bike." She graduated from the Davenport Business School, and formerly worked for Lexicon Music as bookkeeper and purchasing agent. Jean is one of the "Chrismon" makers at New Hope Church.

JOHN SLAGTER, who says he and Jean are 100% Dutch down to their wooden shoes, served his country in WWII in Medical Administration Services. He has retired from his position as Materiels Manager at an aerospace firm in Burbank. (John says the "e" in materiels is most certainly true.) Now he has more time for his hobbies of camping, hiking and cycling. John belongs to the San Fernando Valley Bicycling Assn: and the American Production and Inventory Control Society. He is an Elder at New Hope Church.

PRUDI STEENHOLDT, mother, grandmother, and homemaker, is a member of the Third Reformed Church in Kalamazoo, MI. She and her son, Jeff, are both artists. He works as a professional artist and designed the Legacy House logo.

MARILYN VENEKLASEN STEKETEE grew up in Holland, MI and Phoenix, AZ. She is a housewife, mother, and business partner, having retired from her work as a legal secretary. She and Bob are members of Emmanuel Reformed Church, Paramount, CA, and former members of New Hope Church where she served as Sunday School Superintendent, teacher, choir member and soloist, church secretary and bookkeeper. Her hobbies are traveling, sewing, writing and singing.

BEVERLY PIERCE STROEBEL, housewife and mother, grew up in Beauford, address Good Thunder, MN. She is a graduate of Mankato State Teachers' College/University in Home Economics and Business. Bev is an organist, choir member and Elder of New Hope Church. Her hobbies are sewing and traveling. She is Development Director for Legacy House. She is of English, Austrian and American Indian heritage.

JANE STROEBEL, the youngest Stroebel daughter, is a Senior at Seattle Pacific University majoring in Computer Science and English. Keeping an ancient VW Bug wired together takes up any spare time that she has.

WILLIAM STROEBEL, of German heritage, is a graduate of Mankato State (B.S.) and the U. of Chicago (M.A.) in Geography. He promised Bev they would see the world and that has been partially fulfilled by living in numerous locations in the U.S., Germany, and a trip to the Orient. Bill works as a Project System Requirements Analyst for Unisys Corp. He is Executive Director of Legacy House, a member and Elder of New Hope Church and a Bethel Bible teacher.

MILDRED STURGEON has moved to Dodge City, KS, leaving a large group of people in California who miss her good humor and talents. She is a victim of ataxia, but faithfully and courageously serves God. She is a retired journalism teacher, a widow, mother and grandmother.

SUE STROEBEL TAMAOKA, housewife and graduate of Cal State, Chico, is a staff member, along with her husband, Scott, of Campus Crusade for Christ, Japan. They are members of New Hope Church.

PEGGY TAYLOR, housewife and mother, serves God as Youth Education Coordinator at New Hope Church. She continues to work on her education at Pierce College, works as a dental assistant and bakes and decorates wonderful cakes. Her favorite vacation spot is Hawaii.

SHANNON TAYLOR, age 12½, attends a San Fernando Valley Christian School and is a member of New Hope Church. She is a good student and aspiring artist who has blessed all of us in this book. (Thank you, Shannon!)

HARLENE THOMAS was born in Chicago, IL, and graduated from Hyde Park High School. Housewife, mother of three, her number 12 grandchild is on the way. Harlene serves on the Board of the West Valley Christian Women's Club and hostesses Friendship Bible Coffees. She is a member of New Hope Church.

EMOGENE TOKUNAGA, wife, mother of two children, and grandmother, was born in Cotton County, OK. When she was seventeen, she moved to San Diego. For twenty-eight years she worked for Safeway in the meat dept. After early retirement, Gene and her husband, Sam, moved to Oklahoma. Later, Sam and Gene moved to Canoga Park, CA, to do evangelism, visitation and serve as property caretakers. "I love to see this place beautiful every minute," expresses Gene's concern for New Hope which is reflected in her work.

KAREN YOUNGSMA VAN ZEE, housewife and mother, is a Child Evangelism teacher, Bible student and member of a church located in Camarillo, CA. She is of Dutch heritage. Her parents are members of New Hope Church.

DANNY WALL, 13, was born in Colorado. Currently he attends El Camino Real High School, Woodland Hills, CA. Reading and camping are his favorite hobbies when he isn't busy at New Hope Church, which he attends with his family. He is also busy with Boy Scout activities. His rank is Life Scout and he's working toward Eagle. He belongs to the Order of the Arrow. Many of the pictures in this book are his work.

LOIS E. WATTS, housewife, mother, and grandmother, attended William Penn College and CSUN. She is a Bible student and presently attends the First Baptist Church of Salem, OR.

WILMA WEBB, a niece of Mildred Sturgeon, is also from Kansas. She and her husband have one son. She works in the accounting field. Her hobbies are poetry writing and sewing. She and her husband are members of St. John's United Methodist Church, Albuquerque, NM.

GEORGETTE WEIRAUCH, of German and Romanian heritage, housewife and mother, is a graduate of Queens College, NY. Her family left Romania as refugees during WWII. They spent the war in Austria and came to the U.S. in 1953, where she met her husband who came from Transylvania. Georgette is a former principal of the German School of Van Nuys which met at New Hope Church for a time. She provided the German translation of the "Invitation." Her hobbies are gardening, traveling and volunteering.

LORRAINE HOPE WILKINSON, housewife, mother, and grandmother, attended Western Michigan University and graduated from CSUN (B.A.) in Communicative Disorders. She is a member and Elder of New Hope Church and serves as organist, choir member and Bible study leader and coordinator. Lori is Production Manager for Legacy House. Her hobbies are music and sewing, and she is a licensed Amateur Radio operator.

ROBERT WILKINSON is also a licensed Amateur Radio operator along with his hobbies of photography and experimental gardening techniques. He is a Lead Design Engineer, member of New Hope Church and Business Manager of Legacy House.

STEVE WILKINSON, husband and father, is a graduate of Azusa Pacific University in music. He is an arranger, composer and free lance musician. Steve is also on the music staff of Calvary Community Church, Agoura Hills, CA.

DEAN YOUNGSMA, husband and father, a former student of Central Bible College, is now a Berean Bible School student. He serves as worship leader in a preaching ministry at Santa Rita County Jail. Dean is involved in a World Wide Radio Ministry, "Seek Me Early," at his church, Faith Chapel in Pleasanton, CA.

"For we cannot help speaking about what we have seen and heard."
Acts 4:20

And All God's People Say Amen

INDEX OF COPYRIGHT OWNERS

We gratefully acknowledge the use of the valid copyrights of the following publishers and individuals.

Legacy House

Unless the Lord builds the house, its builders labor in vain.

—Psalm 127:1a

...to prepare God's people for works of service, so that the body of Christ may be built up until we all reach unity in the faith and in the knowledge of the Son of God.

—Ephesians 4:12, 13a

God is spirit, and his worshipers must worship in spirit and in truth.

—John 4:24

BEVERLY PIERCE STROEBEL AND LORRAINE HOPE WILKINSON have been friends and members of the same church since 1960. Their relationship originated from a mutual interest in music as they shared the responsibility of pianist and organist at the Platt Ranch Church. This church later merged with Family Church to become New Hope Community Church in Canoga Park, California.

Their shared musical partnership ended in 1976 when Beverly moved with her family to Germany and resumed upon their return to Los Angeles in 1980. Since then, choir, organ and piano remain a mutual interest and avenue of service.

The Stroebels' three daughters and Wilkinson's two daughters and four sons grew up in the Canoga Park area. All made confession of faith as young people in their parents' church. All nine children, spouses and the Wilkinson grandchildren are frequent visitors in their parents' homes.

A mutual commitment to prayer and Bible study has enriched this continuing friendship, which has led to the development of Legacy House Publishing Company.

Legacy House is built on our faith in the promises of God's Word. Believing the creative power of God speaks through word, music and artistry, Legacy House strives to be a channel for aspiring writers, composers and artists to publish their works.

The invitation to partnership is open to all who seek to express their faith through word, song and artistry for worship in spirit and in truth.

We pledge to give the first fruits of these labors to the Lord's work.

Beverly Pierce Stroebel
Development Director

Lorraine Hope Wilkinson
Production Director

LEGACY HOUSE ORDER FORM

I want to order *IN THE SPIRIT OF CHRISTMAS*.
Please send me _______ copies at $6.95 per copy   = $_____________

(Californians: Please add 6½% sales tax)   = $_____________

$1.25   Shipping   = $_____________
*($1 for the first book and
50¢ for each additional book)*

TOTAL AMOUNT ENCLOSED = $_____________

Payment must accompany order
(Check in U.S. funds only, please)

–Prices confirmed through January 1988–

SHIP TO ____
PRINT NAME

STREET ____

CITY ____

STATE ______________________ ZIP ___________________

Make check payable to:
**LEGACY HOUSE
23815 Northwoods View Road
Canoga Park, CA 91307**

LEGACY HOUSE ORDER FORM

I want to order *IN THE SPIRIT OF CHRISTMAS*.
Please send me _______ copies at $6.95 per copy   = $_______________

(Californians: Please add 6½% sales tax)   = $_______________

$1.25   Shipping   = $_______________
*($1 for the first book and
50¢ for each additional book)*

TOTAL AMOUNT ENCLOSED = $_______________

Payment must accompany order
(Check in U.S. funds only, please)

–Prices confirmed through January 1988–

SHIP TO ____
PRINT NAME

STREET ____

CITY ____

STATE _________________________ ZIP _________________________

Make check payable to:
**LEGACY HOUSE
23815 Northwoods View Road
Canoga Park, CA 91307**